POLITICS & POT ROAST

POLITICS & POT ROAST

An Unofficial, Unauthorized & Completely Unclassified Cookbook

Sarah Hood Salomon

Illustrated by

Glenn Foden

BRIGHT SKY PRESS

BRIGHT SKY PRESS

Box 416
Albany, Texas 76430

10   9   8   7   6   5   4   3   2   1

Library of Congress Cataloging-in-Publication Data

Salomon, Sarah Hood, 1956–
    Politics and pot roast : an unofficial, unauthorized & completely unclassified cookbook / by Sarah Hood Salomon ;
Illustrated by Glenn Foden.
        p. cm.
    Includes bibliographical references and index.
    ISBN-13: 978-1-931721-79-0 (cloth : alk. paper) 1. Cookery. 2. Presidents—United States. I. Title.

    TX714.S23 2006
    641.5—dc22

                                                             2006011983

Book and cover design by Isabel Lasater Hernandez
Edited by Kristine Krueger

Printed in China through Asia Pacific Offset

To my wonderful parents

Who made me feel as if I could do anything

Table of Contents

Acknowledgments 8

Introduction 10

Etiquette Rules for State Dinners 12

★ Washington, George 14

★ Adams, John 20

★ Jefferson, Thomas 24

★ Madison, James 28

★ Monroe, James 32

★ Adams, John Quincy 36

★ Jackson, Andrew 40

★ Van Buren, Martin 44

★ Harrison, William Henry 48

★ Tyler, John 52

★ Polk, James K. 56

★ Taylor, Zachary 60

★ Fillmore, Millard 62

★ Pierce, Franklin 64

★ Buchanan, James 66

★ Lincoln, Abraham 70

★ Johnson, Andrew 76

★ Grant, Ulysses S. 80

★ Hayes, Rutherford B. 84

★ Garfield, James A. 88

★ Arthur, Chester A. 92

★ Cleveland, Grover..................................96

★ Harrison, Benjamin....................100

★ McKinley, William 104

★ Roosevelt, Theodore....................108

★ Taft, William H. 112

★ Wilson, Woodrow 116

★ Harding, Warren G. 120

★ Coolidge, Calvin 124

★ Hoover, Herbert................................128

★ Roosevelt, Franklin D.....................132

★ Truman, Harry 138

★ Eisenhower, Dwight D. 144

★ Kennedy, John F. 150

★ Johnson, Lyndon B. 156

★ Nixon, Richard M. 162

★ Ford, Gerald R. 166

★ Carter, Jimmy 170

★ Reagan, Ronald.................................174

★ Bush, George H.W. 180

★ Clinton, William J. 186

★ Bush, George W. 192

Presidential Nicknames.....................................198
Bibliography 200
Index 204

Acknowledgments

Heartfelt accolades to my husband, Robin, for being so supportive throughout this project. His insightful comments, detailed proofreading and knowledge of history were immensely helpful. He tasted some pretty weird recipes (which did not make it into the cookbook!). He also drove extra carpool trips, washed a lot of dirty dishes and ordered take-out food when I was so busy writing that there wasn't time to cook spaghetti. Hugs and kisses go out to my three wonderful kids, Tory, Tim and Ryan.

Special thanks go to my sister, Corky Hebert, for her willingness to cook almost anything once, and to my brother, Duncan Hood, whose computer wizardry kept the manuscript from being transmitted into cyberspace.

I would also like to thank the good friends who contributed to the preparation and consumption of the recipes. These friends include Fred and Anne Vinson, the McConnells, the Yockeys, Anne Lindgren and Kurt Schluntz, the Blakeys, Lucy McFadden and Marc Allen, the "Ozgurs," the Pfliegers, the Bakers, the Anthonys, the Donoghues, Leslie Healy and Susie Salomon. Gay Barclay and Penny Morrill provided invaluable editing assistance.

Kudos go to the illustrator, Glenn Foden, whose slightly twisted sense of humor kept everyone giggling. I'd also like to acknowledge Kristine Krueger, for her editorial expertise, and Isabel Lasater Hernandez, for the superb layout of the book. My thanks go especially to Rue Judd and the talented people at Bright Sky Press, who made the whole thing possible.

"More than health depends on the proper preparation of food: our very virtues are the creatures of circumstances, and many a man has hardened his heart, or given up a good resolution, under the operation of indigestion. Who that knows the world, ever solicits with confidence a friendly or charitable act of another before dinner."

The Cook's Own Book
by a Boston housekeeper
(Mrs. N.K.M. Lee), 1832

"Whatever the nation, skill in pastry making has been regarded worldwide as a passport to matrimony. In Hungarian villages, for example, no girl was considered eligible until her strudel dough had become so translucent that her beloved could read the newspaper through it. ... pastries must be made the way porcupines make love—that is, very, very carefully."

The Joy of Cooking
by Irma S. Rombauer and
Marion Rombauer Becker, 1981

Introduction

It all started with a "simple" dinner party. Members of the Garden Club of America were coming to Washington, D.C., for a meeting, and I extended an invitation for dinner, assuming there would be only 10 women. Only later did I realize that 30 sophisticated women would be coming to my house expecting to be fed!

I picked a Washington, D.C., theme for the dinner and began researching recipes by U.S. Presidents and First Ladies.

The party began with Ulysses S. Grant's "Roman Punch" and took off from there. The dishes were labeled with their names and creators, which kept the conversation lively. The party was one of the best I'd ever given.

I continued to collect recipes and decided to put them together in a small book. I also hosted several highly successful taste-testing parties. The recipes were combined with anecdotes about each administration, and a softcover version was used as a fund-raiser for Children's Hospital, the Garden Club of America and The Corcoran Gallery. The book went through three printings. I then contacted Bright Sky Press, which agreed to publish this expanded and illustrated edition.

Many of the recipes are original, and some are favorites of the Presidents and First Ladies. The name of the President or First Lady is included in the recipe title if the authorship is believed to be original. For example, "Elizabeth Monroe's Syrup of Roses" is an authentic recipe.

When verifiable recipes were not available, I sought to make connections between the Presidents and the chosen dishes. Menus from State Dinners or references to favorite foods were used, and recipes were then taken from cookbooks of that era.

For example, "Maids of Honor" is from *The White House Cook Book,* published in 1887. It contains recipes compiled in part by Hugo Ziemann, steward of the White House during Grover Cleveland's administration. Cleveland was the only President to be married in the White House, so "Maids of Honor" seemed appropriate for the section about him.

First Lady Lucy Hayes was nicknamed "Lemonade Lucy" because all alcohol was banned from the White House during her husband's presidency. The Rutherford B. Hayes Presidential Center provided the name of a cookbook owned by Mrs. Hayes, *Practical Cooking and Dinner Giving,* and I've included the lemonade recipe from that book.

At one time, the jelly roll cake was referred to as "Lincoln's Log." Looking for a connection between the recipe and President Lincoln, I discovered an early version of the "jelly cake" was created by Laura Keene, a British actress who was performing in *Our American Cousin* at Ford's Theatre on the night Lincoln was shot. She was able to identify the assassin, John Wilkes Booth, a fellow actor, though he was not in the production that night.

The question I'm asked most frequently is about the recipe origins. Presidential libraries and homes were an invaluable source of information, and I researched old cookbooks at the Library of Congress. Several earlier books contained recipes of Presidents and First Ladies.

The validity of authorship is sometimes questionable, and there was a common practice of naming dishes after famous people. *Our Own Cook Book,* for example, was published in 1892 by the Ladies of the First Presbyterian Church. The book contains a recipe for "Mrs. Grant's Veal Olives," yet the First Lady confessed in her memoirs, "... some ladies wanted to get up a cookbook and wrote to me for an original recipe. I did not know what to do ... I was forced to ask the advice of a friend, who advised me to tell these ladies that I did not have an original recipe, did not know much about these matters and had always depended on my cook."

I found many fascinating tidbits of information about food preferences and entertaining styles from each administration, along with fun anecdotes—like the one about the 78-pound watermelon presented to President McKinley.

Some of the stories may have been embellished over the years ... such as the wild party following the inauguration of Andrew Jackson, during which the President was said to have jumped out of a side window to escape the crush of people. At another party, President Van Buren is reported to have run around the room pretending to be a turkey.

Early cookbooks were rare and treasured items. They listed most ingredients but sometimes left out items deemed to be obvious. The books presumed the cook had a basic knowledge and would know to add isinglass to any recipe for a flummery (a type of pudding). Quantities of ingredients were not often given, and the cook would adjust amounts to suit the size of her family. Directions were vague and rarely included baking times or temperatures. A recipe might recommend, "flour enough to make a soft dough," or place cake in a "slack oven" and bake "until enough."

Some old recipes have been updated to reflect modern cooking techniques, but when available, I have included the original versions so you may interpret the recipes in your own fashion.

I have had great fun researching this book, and I hope it brings you much enjoyment. The next time you get invited to someone's house for dinner, instead of giving your host a bottle of wine, offer to bring along some rissables, some petticoat tails, a shrub or a chestnut flummery.

Etiquette Rules for State Dinners

Excerpts from *The White House Cook Book, 1887*

One's teeth are not to be picked at table; but if it is impossible to hinder it, it should be done behind the napkin.

Be careful to keep the mouth shut closely while masticating the food. It is the opening of the lips which causes the smacking which seems very disgusting.

Don't, when you drink, elevate your glass as if you were going to stand it inverted on your nose.... Drink gently, and not pour it down your throat like water turned out of a pitcher.

One may pick a bone at the table, but as with corn, only one hand is allowed to touch it ... to take her teeth to it gives a lady the look of caring a little too much for the pleasures of the table; one is, however, on no account to suck one's finger after it.

The knife should never be used to carry food to the mouth, but only to cut it up into small mouthfuls.

It is not proper to drink with a spoon in the cup; nor should one, by-the-way, ever quite drain a cup or glass.

Spoons are sometimes used with firm puddings, but forks are the better style. A spoon should never be turned over in the mouth.

Never ask to be helped to soup a second time. The hostess may ask you to take a second plate, but you will politely decline. Fish chowder ... is said to be an exception.

There is no position where the innate refinement of a person is more fully exhibited than at the table, and nowhere that those who have not been trained in table etiquette feel more keenly their deficiencies.

To be at ease is a great step towards enjoying your own dinner, and making yourself agreeable to the company. There is reason for everything in polite usage; thus the reason why one does not blow a thing to cool it, it is not only that it is an inelegant and vulgar action intrinsically, but because it may be offensive to others—cannot help being so, indeed; and it, moreover implies, haste, which, whether from greediness or a desire to get away, is equally objectionable.

"One's teeth are not to be picked at table; but if it is impossible to hinder it, it should be done behind the napkin."

☆

George Washington

№ 1

Martha Washington's Great Cake

Original Recipe

Take 40 eggs divide the whites from the yolks & beat them to a froth then work 4 pounds of butter to a cream & put the whites of the eggs to it a Spoon full at a time till it is well work'd then put 4 pounds of sugar finely powdered to it in the same manners then put it in the Youlks [sic] of eggs & 5 pounds of flower [sic] & 5 pounds of fruit. 2 hours will bake it add to it half an ounce of mace & nutmeg half a pint of wine and some frensh [sic] brandy.

Updated Recipe

10 eggs
1 pound butter
1 pound sugar
1¼ pounds flour
1¼ pounds assorted fruit & nuts*
2½ teaspoons ground mace
2½ teaspoons ground nutmeg
2 ounces wine

2 ounces French brandy
Icing (recipe on next page)

Preheat oven to 350° F. Separate egg whites from yolks and set yolks aside. Beat egg whites to a "soft peak." Cream the butter. Slowly add the beaten egg whites, one spoonful at a time, to the butter. Slowly add the sugar, one spoonful at a time. Add egg yolks. Add flour, slowly, and then add fruit.

   Add ground mace and nutmeg, wine and brandy. Lightly grease and flour a 10" springform cake pan. Pour batter into pan and bake about 75 minutes. Allow cake to cool after baking.

   *For assorted fruit & nuts, the following items are suggested based on what would have been available to Mrs. Washington, either fresh or dried (1¼ pounds equals 20 ounces):

9½ ounces of apple (peeled, cored and diced)
5 ounces of pear (peeled, cored and diced)
3½ ounces of raisins
2 ounces of sliced almonds

Modern adaptation of an 18th-century icing

3 egg whites
1½ cups powdered sugar
2 tablespoons orange-flower water
1 teaspoon grated lemon peel

Beat egg whites and 2 tablespoons of powdered sugar. Continue adding sugar in small amounts until you have used all the sugar. Add orange-flower water and lemon peel. Beat until the icing is stiff enough to stay parted when a knife cuts through it. Smooth it onto the cake. Let it dry and harden in 200° F oven for 1 hour. (Note: Icing will be brittle when cut with a knife.)
Recipe courtesy of Mount Vernon, George Washington's Home. *

The President's home at Mount Vernon was famous for hospitality. Visitors were so numerous that Washington became concerned about expenses. He said, "My manner of living is plain, and I do not mean to be put out by it. A glass of wine and a bit of mutton are always ready, and such as will be content to partake of them are always welcome. Those who expect more will be disappointed."

One evening, Washington stood with his back to the fire. When the fire became too hot, he moved away. One guest said a General should stand fire. Washington agreed, but replied that a General shouldn't receive it from behind.

'Gyngerbrede'

Attributed to Mary Washington (President Washington's Mother)

½ cup butter
½ cup brown sugar
1 cup molasses
3 eggs
1½ teaspoons cinnamon
1 teaspoon baking soda
2 tablespoons ground ginger
3 cups flour
1 teaspoon mace
1 teaspoon nutmeg
½ cup orange juice
1 teaspoon orange zest
1 cup buttermilk
1 cup raisins

Cream butter and sugar. Stir in molasses. Add eggs, one at a time, and mix well. Sift the dry ingredients together and set aside. Combine the orange juice, orange zest, buttermilk and raisins and set aside.

Beat ⅓ of the flour mixture into the butter mixture, then add ⅓ of the milk mix. Repeat until all ingredients are combined. Put into greased 9" x 13" pan and bake at 350° F for 50 minutes (or until straw inserted in gingerbread comes out clean). Yields 24 pieces. ✳

Gingerbread is one of the earliest known recipes. The Romans made it over 2,000 years ago. Mary Washington was famous for her gingerbread and often prepared it for visitors. The crusty end piece, which was always cut off, was referred to as the "kissing piece."

Mrs. Washington may have served this dessert at a dinner given to honor General Lafayette when he visited Fredericksburg in 1784. Lafayette later made a triumphant tour of the United States in 1824–25. A recipe called "Lafayette Gingerbread" was published in *Seventy-Five Recipes for Pastry, Cakes and Sweetmeats* by "A Lady of Philadelphia" (Eliza Leslie, 1832). Miss Leslie published several cookbooks; in a book from 1850,

MOTHER of the FATHER OF OUR COUNTRY

she said the recipe was also called "Franklin Gingerbread." Gingerbread was reportedly a favorite of Abraham Lincoln as well.

As a mother, Mary was very domineering and criticized George constantly. Even when her son became President, she didn't appreciate the importance of his accomplishments. She accused him of not properly supporting her and constantly pestered him for more money.

Mount Vernon's Mint Juleps

Handful of fresh mint
1 to 4 tablespoons sugar
⅛ to ½ cup water
Crushed ice (about 1 cup)
½ to 1 cup bourbon
Powdered sugar

Reserve one mint sprig for garnish. Put remaining mint in the bottom of a (tall) glass, and crush with a mortar. Put in simple syrup (made from the sugar and water). Fill with crushed ice. Pour bourbon on top. Dip mint sprig in powdered sugar as garnish. Quantities of the ingredients may be adjusted for individual tastes.

Recipe supplied by the Mount Vernon Ladies Association. ★

☆ Veal and Bacon Pie

11 to 12 ounces pastry dough
¼ pound bacon
1½ pounds veal, cubed
Salt and pepper
4 hard-boiled egg yolks
½ tablespoon parsley
½ teaspoon thyme
½ teaspoon marjoram
½ teaspoon savory
1 uncooked egg white
2 tablespoons butter

Line 9" pie pan with half of the pastry. Cook bacon and crumble over meat. Season with salt and pepper and place into pastry. Mix egg yolks and spices. Bind with egg white and mix with meat. Dot with butter. Put remaining pastry over the top. Bake at 350° F for 1 hour. Serves 8–10.

Recipe adapted from a book written by Frances Parke Custis, mother of Martha Washington's first husband. ★

"I think I am more like a state prisoner than anything else. There [are] certain bounds set for me which I must not depart from. I would much rather be at home."

—*Martha Washington*

Mushrooms in Cream

1 pound mushrooms
4 tablespoons butter
1 small white onion
¾ cup heavy cream
1 tablespoon chopped parsley
½ teaspoon nutmeg
¼ teaspoon salt
Pinch of thyme
Pepper to taste
2 egg yolks

Wash the mushrooms and cut into thick slices. Melt 2 tablespoons butter in medium-size saucepan. Cut the onion in half and place each half face down in pan. Put mushrooms in pan and simmer for 10 minutes, stirring occasionally. Remove onion and add all remaining ingredients except egg yolks.

Cook 5 minutes. Add egg yolks and cook 2 minutes. Serve immediately. Serves 6.

Recipe adapted from a book written by Frances Parke Custis, mother of Martha Washington's first husband. Mrs. Custis gave the book to Martha, who later gave it to her beloved granddaughter, Nellie Custis. ✱

☆ Every Tuesday, President Washington held a "levee," or reception, which was reserved and formal. He disliked shaking hands, feeling it was too familiar, so he stood with one hand on his sword and held his hat in the other hand. He always stood in front of the fireplace, with his head turned toward the door.

At 3 o'clock, each visitor was announced to the President, who bowed politely. At 3:15, the doors were closed and the guests formed a circle. The President went around the room, exchanging words with each visitor. When finished, he resumed his place at the fireplace. Each visitor approached in turn, bowed and left the room. The ceremony was over by 4 o'clock.

Washington held the first recorded barbecue in America. A 500-pound ox was roasted after the President laid the cornerstone for the Capitol. The Senate initially wanted to address Washington as "His Highness the President of the United States of America, and the Protector of Their Liberties." Washington preferred to be called simply "Mr. President."

He started the tradition of giving an inaugural address, although the speech was written mostly by James Madison. After the inauguration, Washington ate lunch alone.

President Washington's salary was $25,000, which is the equivalent of about $1 million today. (Today the President is paid $500,000.)

Mount Vernon's Colonial Peanut and Chestnut Soup ☆

¼ cup margarine
1½ tablespoons all-purpose flour
1 quart chicken broth
1 cup smooth peanut butter
1 tablespoon Worcestershire sauce
1 quart water
½ cup unsalted peanuts, chopped
½ cup water chestnuts, chopped

Melt margarine in a large saucepan. Stir in flour to make a roux. Cook on medium heat while frequently stirring until the roux is light tan in color. Once the roux is ready, add chicken broth (add broth slowly and stir until smooth) and bring to a boil. Stir in peanut butter and Worcestershire sauce. Hold on stove at low heat until ready to serve. The longer it heats, the thicker it gets. (Water may be added if soup gets too thick.) Garnish with chopped peanuts and water chestnuts. Serves 10–12.

Recipe supplied by the Mount Vernon Ladies Association. ★

"I go to the chair of government with feelings not unlike those of a culprit who is going to the place of his execution."

—*George Washington*

John Adams

№ 2

Apple Pan Dowdy

Attributed to Abigail Adams

Pastry
1½ cups flour
½ cup shortening
Dash of salt
Ice water
¼ cup butter

Filling
10 large apples
½ cup sugar
½ teaspoon cinnamon
¼ teaspoon salt
¼ teaspoon nutmeg
½ cup molasses
3 tablespoons butter, melted
¼ cup water

Blend first three pastry ingredients. Sprinkle enough ice water over dough to hold it together. Roll out dough; cut butter into dough. Cut pastry in half. Place halves on top of each other. Roll and cut again. Repeat. Chill for 1 hour.

Roll pastry and cut in half. Use half to line bottom of baking dish. Peel and slice the apples. Mix with sugar and spices; put in pastry-lined dish. Mix molasses, butter and water. Pour over apples. Cover with top crust and seal. Bake at 400° F for 10 minutes. "Dowdy" the dish by cutting crust into the apples with a knife. Bake at 350° F for 1 hour. Serve hot with ice cream or whipped cream. Makes 6 servings. *

John Adams' Recipe to Make a Patriot

Take of the several Species of Malevolence, as Revenge, Malice, Envy, equal Quantities, of servility, fear, fury, Vanity, Prophaneness, and Ingratitude, equal Quantities, and infuse this Composition into the Brains of an ugly, surly, brutal Mortal and you have the Desideratum.

John Adams' Diary,
9 February 1763

Meat Pasties

1 pound (about 4 cups) cooked chicken, beef
    or ham
3 hard-boiled egg yolks
1 tablespoon sugar
¼ teaspoon salt
¼ teaspoon nutmeg
¼ teaspoon ground cloves
1 tablespoon creamy mustard
Puff pastry
Egg, lightly beaten

Chop meat into very small pieces and set aside.
Mash egg yolks, then combine with sugar, spices
and mustard. Add the meat and mix together with
hands. Lay out a sheet of puff pastry. Pasties may be
made into appetizers or individual serving portions.

For appetizers, cut pastry into 3-inch squares. Put
about ½ tablespoon of meat mixture in one corner.
Fold one corner to the opposite corner, making a
triangle that encompasses the filling. Pinch sides
together to seal. Repeat until all meat mixture is used.

For individual servings, cut pastry into 8-inch
squares. Put about ⅓ cup of meat mixture in one
corner of pastry.

Fold one corner to the opposite corner, making a
triangle that encompasses the filling. Pinch sides
together to seal. Repeat until all meat mixture is used.

 Place pasties on greased cookie sheets. Brush
top of each pasty with egg. Bake at 375° F for
15–20 minutes or until golden. Yields about 30
appetizers or 6 individual servings.

Recipe adapted from *The House-Keeper's Pocket-Book*, 1755, which may have been owned by the Adams family. ★

Although *The House-Keeper's Pocket-Book* was
an English cookbook, colonists and early
Americans used it because at that time, there
were no published American recipe books.
Another popular English cookbook was *The Art
of Cookery Made Plain and Easy*, written by a
man who used the pen name Hanna Glasse.

On the Fourth of July, President and Mrs.
Adams hosted a grand party for Members of
Congress, the Governor, local officials and
military personnel. Long tables were set up on
the lawn of the mansion, and over 200 pounds
of cake were consumed.

"Did you ever see a portrait of a great man without
perceiving strong traits of pain and anxiety?"

—John Adams

A Nice Indian Pudding

Salt a pint meal, wet with one quart milk, sweeten and put into a strong cloth, brass or bell metal vessel, stone or earthen pot, secure from wet and boil 12 hours.

> Recipe from *American Cookery* by Amelia Simmons, 1796, believed to be the first American cookbook. *

The Hasty Pudding

The yellow flour, bestrew'd and stirr'd with haste,
Swells in the flood and thickens to a paste,
Then puffs and wallops, rises to the brim,
Drinks the dry knobs that on the surface swim;
The knobs at last the busy ladle breaks,
And the whole mass its true consistence takes.
Could but her sacred name, unknown so long,
Rise, like her labours, to the son of song,
To her, to them, I'd consecrate my lays,
And blow her pudding with the breath of praise.

> Excerpt from "The Hasty Pudding" by Joel Barlow, written in Chambery, in Savoy, January 1793.

☆ Hasty Pudding

Updated Recipe

3 cups milk
4 tablespoons cornmeal
¼ cup butter
4 eggs, lightly beaten
1 cup raisins
1 teaspoon cinnamon
½ teaspoon nutmeg
¼ cup sugar
Pinch of salt

Pour milk into saucepan and scald over medium heat. Slowly stir in cornmeal. Cook 5 minutes over low heat. Mix well, then remove from heat. Add butter and stir. Cool, then mix in remaining ingredients. Pour into greased 8" x 8" pan. Bake 2 hours at 300° F, and then put in individual serving cups. Make well in center and put in butter or syrup. Serves 8. *

Hasty Pudding is a variation of Indian Pudding, but it required much less time. The old-fashioned Indian Pudding was boiled for 12 hours in a waterproof sack. In Colonial times, puddings were often unsweetened and served before the meat course to help fill empty stomachs. They were made with corn, rice, potatoes, vegetables, or fruits.

John Adams was said to have read the Bible cover to cover every year. Abigail rose at 5 a.m., and she read, wrote letters and prayed until 8 a.m. The family then had breakfast together.

President Adams moved into the White House four months before losing the election to Jefferson. The mansion was unfinished, drafty and cold. The central staircase was not yet finished, and an outhouse stood next to the mansion, until Jefferson later installed water closets. Abigail described it as "a house on a grand scale," but said it "stood on a desolate bog. There were no bathrooms ... water had to be carried by hand from a distance of five city blocks ... and the great unfinished audience room (East Room) I made a drying room of (for laundry)."

When Adams first moved into the White House, Abigail stayed behind to pack, so her husband wrote her a prayer, which Franklin Roosevelt later had inscribed on the fireplace in the State Dining Room:

I pray Heaven to Bestow
The Best of Blessings on
THIS HOUSE
and on All that shall hereafter
Inhabit it. May none but Honest
and Wise Men ever rule under this Roof!

They held the first White House reception in 1800. Since the first floor was uninhabitable, the party was held on the second floor. Twenty cords of wood were burned in a vain attempt to heat the reception room. Following the pattern set by Washington, President and Mrs. Adams were on a raised platform. Adams bowed to each guest, while his wife remained seated next to him.

"My residence in this city has not served to endear the world to me. I am sick, sick and sick of publick [sic] life."

—*Abigail Adams*

Thomas Jefferson

№ 3

Jefferson may be the greatest Renaissance man this country will ever know. He was a connoisseur of fine wine and food, and he considered the dishes served and the company at your table to be the mark of a civilized man. During his service as minister to France, he developed a love of French cuisine and brought back many recipes from Paris. He also retained a taste for American foods and grew Virginia sweet corn in his Paris garden.

While in France, he tasted a superior type of Italian rice. He crossed the Alps and went to Italy to find where it was grown. Exporting the seed was a crime punishable by death, but Jefferson stuffed his pockets with seeds and bribed a mule driver to carry some in bags. He then smuggled it into the United States, where it is still grown today.

Washington, D.C., was a little backwater town in Jefferson's time. He wanted to bring the level of sophistication closer to Europe's, so he began having concerts at the White House. He introduced many gourmet items to America, including vanilla and Baked Alaska. Whenever he tasted a dish he liked, Jefferson relentlessly badgered the chef into giving him the recipe.

Macaroons

1½ cups blanched almonds
1 cup sugar
¼ teaspoon salt
2 egg whites
1 teaspoon butter

Place almonds, sugar and salt in a food processor and chop very fine. Beat egg whites until foamy and fold gently into the almond mixture. Butter a large sheet of parchment paper and use it to line a baking sheet. Drop the batter by teaspoonfuls onto the parchment. Bake in the middle of a 300° F oven for 15–20 minutes or until cookies are golden around the edges. Let them cool, then peel the macaroons from the paper and store in an airtight container.

Updated version of a recipe that Jefferson brought back from Paris. ★

"Whenever a man has cast a longing eye on offices, a rottenness begins in his conduct."
—*Thomas Jefferson*

Veal Cutlets in Papers

Original Recipe

Take 2 pounds of veal cutlet, in 2 cutlets, and flatten well. Butter a sheet of paper, sprinkle with bread crumbs, mushrooms, and herbs chopped very fine. Salt and pepper.

   This is one of many recipes collected by Thomas Jefferson and used at Monticello.

Updated Recipe

2 pounds veal cutlets
Salt and pepper to taste
1 teaspoon fresh thyme
1 cup bread crumbs
1 pound mushrooms
¼ cup butter
6 squares parchment paper (12 inches)
Additional butter, melted

Trim fat and gristle from veal. Pound cutlets until thin. Mix salt, pepper, thyme and bread crumbs in a small bowl. Press veal into bread crumb mixture until all sides are coated; set aside. Wash and slice mushrooms. Melt butter in a pan and sauté mushrooms until tender.

   Brush parchment paper with melted butter; place a cutlet in the center of each square. Put equal amounts of mushrooms on each piece. Gather up edges of paper and twist together at top. Secure with twine or kitchen string. Place on cookie sheet and bake at 375° F for 45 minutes. Put on individual plates and let guests open packets themselves. Serves 6. *

Jefferson had been a widower for 19 years when he became President. His daughter Martha and James Madison's wife, Dolley, often acted as hostesses. Jefferson preferred small intimate dinners and seated his guests around an oval table so everyone could talk. He limited the number of large public receptions to New Year's Day and the Fourth of July.

Jefferson also did away with the custom of having one waiter for every one or two guests. He thought this crowded the room and gave the servants opportunities to overhear conversations. His invention of the dumbwaiter allowed the food to be loaded onto shelves in the kitchen. The shelves rotated through a cutout area of the wall, and guests then served themselves.

The American Revolution signaled the dawn of a new democracy. To Jefferson, this also meant that the trappings of royalty had to be discarded. He refused to wear a powdered wig and sometimes even greeted foreign dignitaries in his pajamas.

Vegetable Chartreuse

4 to 5 large carrots
1 large potato
1 small bunch asparagus
1 14-ounce jar artichoke hearts
4 slices bacon, cooked
3 eggs
1/8 teaspoon mace
1/4 teaspoon nutmeg
Salt and pepper to taste
1/4 cup sour cream

Peel and slice carrots into thin strips. Steam until tender. Peel potato and cut into quarters. Boil until tender, then cut into thin slices. Steam asparagus until just tender. Slice artichoke hearts.

Grease a deep 9" or 10" circular pan. Line the bottom and sides of pan with asparagus spears and carrots. Add a layer of potato slices and sprinkle with crumbled bacon. Place artichoke hearts and any remaining vegetables into pan "in a fanciful way." Lightly beat eggs and then stir in spices and sour cream; pour over vegetables. Lay a piece of buttered parchment over the top.

Put pan in a large baking pan. Add 1/2 inch of water to the baking pan. Bake at 350° F for 1 hour or until done. Remove circular pan from larger pan, and loosen edges of Chartreuse. Let it cool for 5 minutes, then invert onto serving platter. Serves 6–8. Updated version of a recipe collected by Jefferson and used at Monticello. ✱

Jefferson ate very little meat and attributed his long life to the abundance of vegetables in his diet. He collected seeds from friends and cultivated many types of plants. Lewis and Clark brought back many plant cuttings from their expedition for Jefferson.

He regarded wine and olive oil as necessities of life and tried unsuccessfully to establish them at Monticello. His favorite vegetable was the pea, and he grew more than 30 varieties. Menus varied according to the season and the availability of fresh fruits and vegetables.

In an 1819 letter to Dr. Vine Utley, he wrote, "I have lived temperately, eating little animal food, and that not as an aliment, so much as a condiment for the vegetables which constitute my principal diet."

"Never did a prisoner, released from his chains, feel such relief as I shall on shaking off the shackles of power."

—*Thomas Jefferson*

Jefferson adored his grandchildren and showered them with gifts. One Christmas, all six grandchildren came to the White House, and the President gave a party for 100 children. The youngsters played games and danced to the music of Jefferson's violin. He entertained them by showing how his pet mockingbird walked up the stairs with him and took food from his lips.

Living in Paris for a number of years, Jefferson had become accustomed to the delicacies available there. When Jefferson returned to the United States, he missed many of the European foods. His confidential secretary, William Short, stayed in Paris and acted as *chargé d'affaires*. Jefferson sent detailed letters to Short, instructing him to send ingredients and items not available in America. Jefferson imported a waffle iron, and he had Short make a special trip to Naples to purchase a "macaroni mold."

Macaroni

Break macaroni in small pieces, there should be 2 cupfuls, and boil in salted water until tender. Grate ¼ pound cheese and mix with the same amount of butter. Stir into the macaroni and bake like polenta. Bake at 350° F for 25 minutes or until cheese melts.

Recipe collected by Jefferson and used at Monticello. ★

James Madison

№ 4

J ames Madison was a Congressman from Virginia at the time of his marriage to Dolley. He was 17 years older, but she said, "Our hearts understand each other."

He had a brilliant mind and wrote most of the Constitution. Jefferson considered him "the greatest man in the world." Madison was the shortest President (he was 5-foot-4) and was somewhat uncomfortable at receptions. However, he had a quick wit. "We sat in a little group close together and took our coffee while we talked," said Margaret Bayard Smith. "Some of Mr. M's anecdotes were very droll, and we often laughed very heartily."

In contrast, Dolley was 5-foot-9. Plus, she often wore high heels and tall, fashionable turbans in her hair, so she stood out in a crowd. Smith described her as having "unassumed dignity, sweetness, grace. It seems to me that such manners would disarm envy itself and conciliate even enemies."

President Madison's Favorite Whiskey Sours

4 lemons
½ pint water
⅓ cup sugar (more to taste)
1 pint aged bourbon whiskey (100 proof)

Squeeze juice from the lemons and set aside. Boil water, sugar and lemon rinds for 3 minutes. Cool. Add lemon juice and bourbon. Taste, adding a little more sugar if needed, and refrigerate at least 12 hours. Remove rinds and squeeze dry. Strain and bottle.

Recipe courtesy of Montpelier, the Madison home in Virginia. A Madison family descendant supplied the recipe, noting that it is supposed to produce the same whiskey sours served at the White House during Madison's tenure. ★

Raspberry Vinegar

To every pint of best white wine vinegar put a pound of fruit. The next day strain the liquor upon the same quantity of fruit, and the following day do the same, but do not squeeze the fruit, only drain the liquor as dry as you can, put it into a stone jar with a pound of sugar to every pint of juice, stir when melted, put it on the fire, let it simmer and skim it. When cold, bottle it and use no glazed or metal vessel for it.

From the Dolley Madison Papers
in the Library of Congress. *

Although Dolley Madison was arguably America's most famous hostess, no original recipes of hers have been recovered. This vinegar recipe, found in her papers in the Library of Congress, is dated 1817, but it is not in Dolley's handwriting.

The earliest known mention of a recipe by Mrs. Madison is found in Allen C. Clark's *Life and Letters of Dolley Madison* 1914. Mr. Clark states that her papers contain "… prescriptions to cure the ailments and recipes to please the palate. Of the latter is her recipe for Sponge Cake:

"One lb. flour, One dozen eggs, One and a half lbs. Sugar, The juice of two lemons and the rind of three grated."

☆ Spoon Bread

1 quart milk
½ teaspoon salt
1 cup cornmeal
3 tablespoons butter
3 eggs, beaten

Scald milk and stir in salt. Sprinkle in cornmeal *very* slowly, stirring until mixed. Cook, uncovered, in a double boiler for 1 hour. Remove from heat and add butter and eggs. Mix well. Pour into a 9" x 13" pan. Bake at 350° F between 45 minutes to 1 hour, or until a straw inserted into the middle comes out clean. *

Spoon bread is one of the earliest American foods. Native Americans showed the settlers at Jamestown how to grind corn and make it into bread. With a consistency similar to pudding, this dish should be served from the baking pan with a spoon—thus, spoon bread. President Madison loved it and ate it almost every day.

"The essence of Government is power; and power, lodged as it must be in human hands, will ever be liable to abuse."

–*James Madison*

When the Madisons moved into the Executive Mansion, it was practically empty. Jefferson had brought his own furniture, which he took back to Monticello when his second term expired. Congress appropriated $26,000 for furnishings. Unfortunately, all of this burned to ashes when the British torched the mansion in 1814.

Dolley had been preparing for a dinner party when the British invaded Washington—she fled from the White House only hours before. She took with her a copy of the Declaration of Independence, a clock, the household silver and the extravagantly expensive red velvet curtains. She also managed to take Gilbert Stuart's portrait of George Washington. The frame had been screwed to the wall, so the frame had to

be broken and the portrait rolled up for easier transportation.

When the British arrived at the mansion, they sat down to eat the dinner that had been prepared, during which Rear Admiral Cockburn made a toast to Madison. After dinner, they ransacked the mansion and set it on fire. The Admiral took two souvenirs: one of Madison's hats and a chair cushion (so that he could remember Mrs. Madison's seat). A thunderstorm eventually put out the blaze, but the mansion was heavily damaged. The Madisons lived in the nearby Octagon House for the remainder of his administration.

Brandy Peaches

Peel your Peaches & put them in a Stone Pot, set the Pot into a Vessel of Water and let it boil until a Straw will pierce the Fruit, then make a Syrup of Brandy & Sugar, one Pound of Sugar to a Quart of Brandy, put in your Peaches. They will be fit for use in a Month. Brown Sugar will do very well. (Better without peeling.) —St. G.T.

This recipe, called "Brandy Peaches— Mrs. Madison," was contained in a letter written by St. George Tucker, of Williamsburg, to his daughter, Mrs. Frances Coalter, February 6, 1804. ✶

Petticoat Tails

Original Recipe

Sift together several Times five Cups of Flour and one Cup of fine powdered Sugar. Cut and knead into this two Cups of Butter. Shape the Dough in Rolls and chill overnight. Slice thin and bake in moderate Oven.

Recipe provided by Market Square Tavern Kitchen, Sparta, Virginia, 1937.

Updated Recipe

5 cups flour
1 cup powdered sugar
2 cups butter, softened
1 teaspoon vanilla
Pinch of salt

Sift together the flour and sugar. Mix all ingredients thoroughly. Shape dough into a roll about 2 inches in diameter. Chill dough overnight. Slice dough thinly and bake on greased cookie sheets at 350° F for 8–10 minutes. ★

 Ice cream was a new and exotic treat in America in the late 1700s and early 1800s. Here is one guest's description of a dinner at the mansion: "Mrs. Madison always entertained with Grace and Charm, but last night there was a sparkle in her eye that set astir an Air of Expectancy among her Guests. When finally the brilliant Assemblage—America's best—entered the dining room, they beheld a Table set with French china and English silver, laden with good things to eat, and in the Centre high on a silver platter, a large shining dome of pink Ice Cream."

Dolley was raised a devout Quaker, but her friendly nature and quick wit made her a legendary hostess. She revived the custom of weekly receptions. Known as "Mrs. Madison's Drawing Rooms," these levees became opportunities for bringing political opponents together. Washington Irving said she was "... a fine, portly buxom dame, who has a smile and a pleasant word for everybody."

During Madison's long political career, their home was open to many foreign dignitaries and members of government. A foreign visitor once criticized Dolley for serving such a plethora of food. She replied, "The profusion of my table so repugnant to foreign customs arises from the happy circumstances of abundance and prosperity in our country."

☆

James Monroe

№ 5

James Monroe was a hardworking and good-natured man, although he dressed in a somewhat old-fashioned way. He wore britches, a buff coat, a wig and a tricornered hat. Thomas Jefferson said his good friend Monroe was "... a man whose soul might be turned wrong side outward, without discovering a blemish to the world."

Elizabeth Monroe was an elegant society woman of great beauty, although she was somewhat aloof. At their last levee on New Year's Day 1825, a guest described Mrs. Monroe: "Her dress was superb black velvet, neck and arms bare and beautifully formed ... her hair in puffs and dressed high on the head and ornamented with white ostrich plumes ... around her neck an elegant pearl necklace. Though no longer young, she is still a very handsome woman."

Elizabeth Monroe's Syrup of Roses

Infuse three pounds of damask rose leaves in a gallon of warm water, in a well-glazed earthen pot with a narrow mouth, for eight hours. Stop so close that none of the virtue may exhale. When they have infused so long, heat the water again, squeeze them out and pour in three pounds more of rose leaves to infuse, for eight hours more; then press them out very hard. To every quart of this infused add four pounds of sugar and boil to a syrup. A syrup such as this would have been poured over fresh fruit or other desserts.

Recipe courtesy of Ash Lawn-Highland, the Monroe home in Virginia. *

Monroe Family Waverly Jumbles

Original Recipe

One pound of flour; one-half pound of butter; three-fourths pound of brown sugar; two eggs; one-half teaspoon of nutmeg; two tablespoons of rose water. Roll out long and cut into strips; join into rings and bake.

Updated Recipe

½ pound butter
2 cups light brown sugar, firmly packed
2 eggs
2 tablespoons rose water or vanilla
½ teaspoon nutmeg
4 cups flour

Cream butter and sugar until well mixed. Add eggs and flavorings and beat again. Stir in flour. Chill dough for at least 1 hour. Pull off a piece of dough and roll it into a rope shape. Join the ends of the rope together to make a circle. Repeat until all dough is used up. Bake at 350° F for 10–12 minutes. Yields about 5 dozen cookies.

Recipe courtesy of Ash Lawn-Highland, the Monroe home in Virginia. ★

 When Monroe became President, the White House was still under repair from the fire set during the War of 1812. The mansion was rebuilt at a cost of $500,000, a staggering sum for the new Republic. Congress appropriated only $50,000 for the refurnishing. Mrs. Monroe lavishly redecorated the mansion with ornate French furniture.

There was not enough money to redo everything, and the East Room remained unfurnished. James Fenimore Cooper, a frequent guest, described one reception this way: "We reached the White House at nine. The court (or grounds) was filled with carriages, and the company was arriving in great numbers. On this occasion two or three additional drawing rooms were opened, though the frugality of Congress has prevented them from finishing the principal reception room of the building."

"We are all liable to error, and those who are engaged in the management of public affairs are more subject to excitement and to be led astray by their particular interests and passions than the great body of our constituents, who ... are calm but deeply interested spectators of events and of the conduct of those who are parties to them."

—*James Monroe*

Elizabeth Monroe's Cucumber Pickles

Two hundred small cucumbers. Use one gallon of vinegar. Three pounds of brown sugar, one ounce of allspice, one-half ounce of cloves, one and one-half ounces of celery seed. Four small red pepper pods, one small cup of whole black pepper. After the cucumbers have been in cold brine a week, wash off and put in a kettle a layer of grape leaves or green cabbage leaves, then a layer of cucumbers. Drop in small pieces of alum and boil until tender in half vinegar and water. Wipe dry, put in airtight jars and pour over the boiling vinegar. Brine for the above—one cup salt to two quarts of water. Delicious!

Recipe courtesy of Ash Lawn-Highland, the Monroe home in Virginia. ∗

During their time in the White House, Mrs. Monroe was not in good health, so she only attended the most essential functions. Washington society resented Mrs. Monroe for not paying or receiving social calls. Some women snubbed her and few would attend functions at the White House. As a result, only men attended the regular gatherings.

 Maria Monroe was the first daughter of any President to be married in the White House. Attended only by family and a few friends, the ceremony probably took place in the Blue Room. The crystal chandelier held 50 candles and was entwined with satin fabric. Mrs. Monroe wore a velvet dress and adorned her hair with an ostrich feather.

Members of Washington society were outraged that they were not invited to the wedding, and there was a virtual boycott of the weekly drawing rooms (receptions). Mrs. William Seaton noted, "The drawing room of the President was opened last night to a beggarly row of empty chairs. Only five females attended, three of whom were foreigners."

Over time, the public couldn't resist the draw of the White House, but the mansion lacked the gaiety of the Madison years.

While Monroe was in office, the cuisine was French and the dinner hour was changed from 4 o'clock to 6 o'clock. One account said, "... French cooking prevailed, much to the disgust of many prominent officials."

The atmosphere in the mansion became very formal and restrained. It was reported that $100 a night was spent on candles.

Monroe Family Mock Turtle Soup

2 cups black beans, soaked overnight in water
 and drained
4 quarts water
½ pound stew beef
½ pound salt pork (bacon may be substituted)
Beef shinbone or ham hock
2 medium onions, chopped fine
2 carrots, grated
1 red pepper pod
Salt and pepper to taste
½ cup port wine
1 lemon, cut into 12 slices
3 hard-boiled eggs, sliced

Place the beans in 4 quarts of water in a large pot.
Add the meat, bones, vegetables and seasonings.
Simmer 4–5 hours. Remove the meat and dice it
fine. Return meat to pot. Cool soup slightly and
then purée. Add port to the soup and reheat
gently. When ready to serve, ladle into soup bowls
and garnish each with a slice of lemon and egg.
Serves 12.

Recipe courtesy of Ash
Lawn-Highland, the
Monroe home in Virginia. ★

Table decorations were lavish, and Mrs.
Monroe purchased gold-plated silverware that
had belonged to Marie Antoinette. "At Mrs.
Monroe's, we had the most stylish dinner I have
been at," said one guest. "The dishes were silver
and set around the waiter (a large tray for
serving food). The plates were handsome china,
the forks ... so heavy that I could hardly lift
them to my mouth ..."

A 13-foot plateau of bronze and mirrors was
used as a centerpiece. Mrs. Monroe decorated the
plateau with wax flowers because it was thought
at the time that fresh flowers dispensed harmful
vapors and depleted the oxygen in a room.

John Quincy Adams

№ 6

John Quincy Adams had served under all five previous Presidents, so he and Mrs. Adams were at ease at European courts as well as American receptions. Louisa Adams was an intelligent woman and accomplished hostess. A verse of the time reflects the public view:

> *"Belles and Matrons, maids and madams,*
> *all are gone to Mrs. Adams."*

The drawing room receptions were so popular that at times the guests seemed to be lifted off their feet and carried along with the crowd. A 19th-century writer described one reception: "The company is treated with coffee, tea, and a variety of cakes, jellies, ice-cream and white and red wine ... all of which are carried about the room amongst the guests upon large trays by servants dressed in livery; each one takes from it what he pleases, when an opportunity offers, which at some of the fullest levees, may not happen very often, not because there is any scarcity of refreshment, but the difficulty the waiters have in making their way through the crowd with their trays ..."

The President, who found these receptions a bore, wrote, "This evening was the sixth drawing room. Very much crowded; 16 senators, perhaps 60 members of the House of Representatives and multitudes of strangers, among whom were the Institutors of Deaf and Dumb from Philadelphia, New York and Hartford. The heat was oppressive, and these parties are becoming more and more insupportable to me."

Plum Pudding

¾ pint flour
½ pint milk
6 ounces suet
½ pound currants
A little nutmeg
2 spoonfuls treacle

To be boiled for 4.

Handwritten by Louisa Adams, who got the recipe from ladies she met in St. Petersburg, while her husband was minister to Russia. Recipe supplied by the Adams National Historical Park. ★

Kisses for a Slack Oven ☆

3 egg whites
1 cup sugar
¼ teaspoon cream of tartar
Dash of salt
1 teaspoon vanilla
Red and green food coloring

Beat egg whites until they hold a soft peak. Continue beating and gradually add sugar. Add cream of tartar, salt and vanilla. Beat until it will hold stiff peaks. Divide into two halves. Add cochineal (red food coloring) to one half and spinach juice (green food coloring) to the other.

Cover cookie sheet with parchment paper. Drop meringues onto sheet using a tablespoon. Bake in a slack oven (275° F) for 30 minutes or until light tan in color. Peel off parchment paper and cool on a rack. Yields about 2 dozen meringues. *

John and Louisa had three sons, John, George and Charles. John is the only President's son to be married in the White House. The bride was his cousin Mary Catherine Helen. Her beauty and flirtatious manner won the heart of each Adams boy.

She was initially engaged to George, but while he was studying law in Boston, Mary began flirting with Charles. John was the handsomest son and the next target for Mary's affections. Mrs. Adams became alarmed at their behavior and insisted Mary break her engagement to George. Soon afterward, Mary and John were married in the oval drawing room. Neither George nor Charles attended the ceremony.

Adams was considered to be somewhat of a slob ... he even wore the same hat for 10 years. He also once owned a pet alligator, which was given to him by General Lafayette. The alligator resided in a bathtub during its brief stay at the White House.

Election Cake

Original Recipe

10 pounds flour
8 pounds butter
4 pounds sugar
29 eggs
3 pints yeast
1½ pints new milk
Cinnamon, nutmeg and a few cloves

Yields 40–50 servings. (Note: Early recipes only listed ingredients, not cooking directions. The cook was supposed to know what to do.)

Recipe from a 1795 manuscript by a Mrs. Dalrymple of Salem, Massachusetts.

Updated Recipe

1 cup milk
1 packet of yeast
2 tablespoons warm water
4 cups flour
1¼ cups sugar
1 teaspoon cinnamon
1 teaspoon nutmeg
½ teaspoon cloves
Pinch of salt

 ½ cup butter
2 eggs
1 cup currants
½ cup port wine

Scald milk in the top of a double boiler. Dissolve yeast in warm water. Add to milk. Sift 1 cup of flour and ¼ cup sugar together; stir into milk mixture. Beat until smooth. Cover bowl with a cloth and set in a warm place.

When it has doubled in size (about 1–2 hours), remove cloth. Sift remaining flour with spices and salt. Cream together butter and remaining sugar. Gradually add eggs and flour mixture and beat until smooth. Beat in yeast/milk mixture. Stir in currants and port wine.

Place in a well-greased 9" x 5" loaf pan. Cover and let rise until doubled in size (about 4–6 hours). Bake at 375° F for 45–55 minutes or until a straw inserted in middle comes out clean. ∗

Election cakes predate the American Revolution. They were made for Election Day, when townspeople gathered together to vote for local officials. They were also made for Muster Day or Training Day, when the men practiced military drills, and the women got together to shop and visit.

Boston Baked Beans

2½ cups canned Great Northern beans
¼ cup brown sugar
1 tablespoon molasses
⅓ cup catsup
⅓ cup chopped red pepper
5 to 6 strips bacon

Place beans, sugar, molasses, catsup and red pepper in an ovenproof casserole dish; mix well. Put bacon strips on top. Cover and bake at 350° F for 30 minutes. Remove cover and bake for another 30 minutes. ∗

Adams was born just outside of Boston, a city famous for its baked beans. This dish was traditionally served on Saturday night, and leftovers were served with codfish cakes for Sunday breakfast. In Colonial times, the recipe would have called for pea beans to be soaked overnight, then baked for 6 or more hours.

☆ As President, Adams was in the habit of early morning skinny-dipping in the Potomac River. One female reporter, Anne Royall, grew frustrated at his refusal to grant her an interview. So one day she went down to the Potomac and sat on his clothes until he agreed to speak with her at a later date—when he was clothed.

On another occasion, Adams had his steward row him and his son John across the Potomac. Mid-river they stripped off their clothes, ready for a swim, but a sudden gust of wind swamped the boat. The men were able to swim to the Virginia shore, and the steward immediately set off for help. It was 3 hours before he returned, and meanwhile, the naked President paced the riverbank or stayed in the river.

Andrew Jackson

№ 7

Rachel Jackson's Famed Grape Salad

Salad
2 pounds seedless green grapes
1 cup chopped celery
½ cup chopped sweet cucumber pickles
Dressing
2 eggs, well beaten
1 cup cider vinegar
½ cup sugar
1 tablespoon butter, well rounded
1 teaspoon mustard
1 teaspoon cornstarch, wet with cream
½ teaspoon salt
½ teaspoon pepper
¾ cup cream

Cut the grapes into halves and blend with the celery and cucumber pickles. Set aside while preparing the dressing. Put all ingredients for dressing, except cream, into a saucepan. Stir until it comes to a boil. Set aside until it cools, stirring occasionally. Beat the cream with a little sugar and stir in last. Pour the dressing into a large serving bowl. Add the grape salad mixture and blend them together. Serve when chilled. ★

President Jackson spent lavish amounts on entertaining. He paid $45,000 for china, silver and furniture, earning him the nickname "King Andrew." He had a horseshoe-shaped table arranged in the State Dining Room. A French chef was hired, and Jackson brought servants up from The Hermitage, his house in Tennessee.

John R. Montgomery described one dinner at the White House. "The table was very splendidly laid and illuminated ... the first course was soup in the French style; then beef bouille, next wild turkey boned and dressed with brains; after that fish, then chicken cold and dressed with white, interlaid with slices of tongue and garnished with dressed salled [sic]; then canvasback ducks and celery; afterwards partridges with sweetbreads, and last pheasants and old Virginia ham."

Emily Donelson often acted as hostess, as Jackson's wife had died three months before he took office. Rachel Jackson suffered a massive stroke and was buried in her inaugural ball gown.

Hedgehog Cookies

½ cup butter
½ cup brown sugar
2 eggs
½ teaspoon baking powder
1¾ cups hickory nuts (or pecans), finely ground
1 cup flour
1 teaspoon vanilla
2 tablespoons cream
½ cup slivered almonds

Cream butter and sugar together in medium-size bowl. Beat eggs lightly and add to butter mixture. Stir in baking powder, ground nuts, flour, vanilla and cream. Beat until smooth. Take about a tablespoon of dough and pat into the shape of a turtle shell. Place on cookie sheet. Put in slivered almonds so they stick out like porcupine quills. Repeat until all dough is used. Bake at 350° F for 15 minutes. Makes about 30 cookies. ✶

"You are uneasy; you never sailed with me before, I see."

—Andrew Jackson

 Jackson loved having his family gathered around him. On quiet evenings, they lit a fire in the parlor. The ladies worked at their sewing while the grandchildren scampered about. Jackson would sit at one end of the room talking with an advisor. He smoked a long reed pipe, which he waved at the children if they became too boisterous.

During his administration, Jackson had the North Portico added to the White House. This became the official entrance to the mansion. He started an orangerie so the White House could have citrus fruits in the winter. In memory of his wife, Rachel, the President planted two magnolia grandiflora trees on the White House grounds. One remains to this day.

Jackson hosted a Christmas party for his grandchildren in 1835. About 100 children were invited to join in games of Blind Man's Buff, Hide-and-Seek and Puss in the Corner. Then the Marine Band struck up a march, and Jackson led the children into the State Dining Room.

A panoply of cakes, pastries and candies was laid out, and in the center of the table was a pyramid of "snowballs." The balls were made out of cotton and covered with starch. When the children pelted each other with them, the snowballs broke apart, showering the children with "snow" and revealing a candy kiss hidden inside.

During the War of 1812, General Jackson defeated the British at the Battle of New Orleans, becoming a national hero. He was known as "Old Hickory" because his troops said he was tough as a hickory tree. For his inauguration, women wore necklaces strung with hickory nuts.

After the inauguration ceremony, a simple reception had been planned. Instead, 20,000 people invaded the mansion, tracking mud onto the carpets and ruining the furniture by standing on it to catch a glimpse of Jackson. The guests broke windows, china and furniture, and a few fights erupted. Jackson scurried out a side window and took refuge in a nearby hotel. One contemporary account said, "... Ladies fainted, men were seen with bloody noses and such a scene of confusion took place as is impossible to describe—those who got in could not get out by the door again but had to scramble out by the windows."

The cooks eventually got people out of the house by putting out tubs of whiskey on the lawn. One particularly memorable gift to the new President was a 1,400-pound block of cheese. As it was eaten, pieces were ground into the carpets by the mob. The odor of the cheese lingered for months.

Sandwiches for Travelers

Spread butter, very thinly, upon the upper part of a stale loaf of bread cut very smooth, and then cut off the slice; now cut off another thin slice, but spread it with butter on the underside, without which precaution the two slices of bread will not fit one another. Next take some cold beef, or ham, and cut it into very minute particles. Sprinkle these thickly over the butter, and, having added a little mustard, put the slices face to face, and press them together. Lastly cut the whole into four equal portions, each of which is to be wrapped in a separate piece of paper.

Recipe from *The Cook's Own Book and Housekeeper's Register* by Eliza Leslie, 1835. This book was owned by the Jackson family. ★

Salad Sauce

1 hard-boiled egg (chopped)
1 raw egg (not recommended)
1 tablespoon water
1 teaspoon salt
1 teaspoon cayenne pepper
1 teaspoon black pepper
1 teaspoon creamy mustard
1 tablespoon vinegar
5 tablespoons cream

The artist, as he styled himself, who invented this salad sauce drove in his carriage to his employer's home and charged them 10 shillings and sixpence for each visit!

Recipe from *The Cook's Own Book and Housekeeper's Register* by Eliza Leslie, 1835. ★

"I know what I am fit for. I can command a body of men in a rough way; but I am not fit to be President."

—Andrew Jackson

 Jackson was a tough and argumentative man who fought in more than 100 duels. His formal education was limited, and he once said, "It's a damn poor mind that can only think of one way to spell a word."

During his time in office, large receptions were sometimes held for as many as 1,000 people. Jessie Benton, daughter of Senator Thomas Benton, had glowing praise for one such event: "I have the beautiful recollection of the whole stately house adorned and ready for the company—the great wood fires in every room, the immense number of wax lights softly burning, the stands of camellias and laurentia banked row upon row."

Cookies

One pound sugar boiled slowly in half pint water, scum well and cool, add two tea spoons pearl ash dissolved in milk, then two and a half pounds flour, rub in 4 ounces butter, and two large spoons of finely powdered coriander seed, wet with above; make roles half an inch thick and cut to the shape you please; bake fifteen or twenty minutes in a slack oven—good three weeks.

This is the first published American recipe for cookies, appearing in *American Cookery* by Amelia Simmons, 1796. ★

Martin Van Buren

№ 8

Salade à la Volaille

2 heads of lettuce, shredded
Salt to taste
Wine vinegar to taste
3 cups sliced cooked chicken
½ cup mayonnaise
½ cup green olives
1 can anchovies
¼ cup capers
5 to 7 artichoke hearts
Watercress for garnish

Put shredded lettuce in a large chilled salad bowl, and season with salt and wine vinegar. Mix sliced chicken with mayonnaise and put on top of lettuce. Decorate with olives, anchovies, capers and artichoke hearts. Garnish with watercress. Toss lightly before serving and place on individual plates. Serves 10. *

Ham Roasted with Madeira

2½-pound ham (fully cooked)
5 carrots, sliced
1 onion, quartered
1 bay leaf
½ teaspoon coriander
¼ teaspoon thyme
1 cup Madeira wine

Place ham in baking pan. Arrange vegetables around the ham. Mix spices into wine and pour over ham. Cover well and place in the refrigerator overnight. Before baking, pour off and reserve Madeira. Roast ham at 325° F for 30 minutes. Pour Madeira over ham and roast an additional 15 minutes, basting occasionally.

Recipe adapted from *The Cook's Own Book and Housekeeper's Register* by Eliza Leslie, 1835. *

Martin Van Buren was a widower, so his daughter-in-law Angelica often served as hostess. Dolley Madison was living in Washington and sometimes performed hostess duties.

After the rowdy public receptions during Jackson's administration, Van Buren closed the White House to the public. Policemen were stationed at the door to keep the "mobocracy" from intruding.

The furniture was in terrible shape from those parties, so Van Buren had a portion of it auctioned off. He personally supervised the redecorations and spent $25,000. He had the oval drawing room redone with blue fabric instead of crimson. The room then became known as the Blue Room.

At one formal dinner, a servant rushed up to Van Buren and said the house was on fire. Van Buren went to the kitchen to put out the flames. When he returned and explained what had happened, his political opponent, Henry Clay, placed his hand on his heart and exclaimed, "I am doing all I can to get you out of this house; but believe me, I do not want to burn you out!"

As a remedy for his chronically irritated stomach, Van Buren drank a tonic of soot, charcoal and water.

☆ Van Buren's Favorite Stewed Beets

12 medium beets
1 scallion, minced
½ teaspoon parsley
⅛ teaspoon salt
⅛ teaspoon pepper
2 tablespoons butter, melted
2 tablespoons vinegar

Put whole beets into a large pot of boiling water. Allow to simmer until nearly done. Drain beets, then skin and slice them. Put slices into a saucepan and add remaining ingredients. Simmer for 20 minutes, stirring occasionally. Serve hot with the pan gravy poured over the top. ∗

"I tread in the footsteps of illustrious men ..."
—*Martin Van Buren*

Pease Pudding (Pea Purée)

1 pound dried peas
3 strips bacon
1 small carrot
2 pieces celery
Salt, pepper and sugar to taste
1 teaspoon nutmeg
2 whole cloves
2 ounces butter
½ cup sour cream

Put the dried peas in a large deep bowl. Cover them with cold water and leave in a cool place overnight. Drain and rinse the peas. Drain again and put peas in a large deep pot with the bacon. Cover with cold water so the water comes up 2 inches above the peas.

   Bring to a boil. Add the vegetables and seasonings. Simmer about 2 hours, until the peas are very soft and the water absorbed, stirring frequently. Remove celery, bacon and cloves. Purée mixture in a blender until smooth. Beat in the butter and sour cream. Adjust seasonings. Arrange in a flat dish and serve hot. Serves 10. ★

Eve's Pudding

If you like a good pudding, mind what you are taught
First take six eggs when they are bought for a groat,
Next take of the fruit that Eve did once cozen,
Well pared and well chopped, at least half a dozen,
Six ounces of bread, let Moll cut the crust,
And let it be crumbled as small as the dust
Six ounces of currants from the stems you must sort,
Lest they break out your teeth and spoil all your sport,
Six ounces of sugar will not be too sweet
Some salt and some nutmeg, the whole will complete
Three hours let it boil without any flutter,
Nor is it quite finished without wine and butter.

   This "recipe" was popular in Scotland and England in the 1790s. It was copied down by a Mrs. Smith of Massachusetts sometime between 1790 and 1831.

"As to the presidency, the two happiest days of my life were those of my entering upon the office and my surrender of it."

—*Martin Van Buren*

Van Buren was born into a middle-class family but aspired to become one of the aristocracy. He gave lavish parties, wore effete clothes and was said to put on airs of being above the common man.

So it is somewhat surprising that at one party, Van Buren reportedly sang a song while standing on one foot. He then ran around the room pretending to be a turkey.

Soon after Van Buren took office, the economy collapsed in the Panic of 1837. Many banks, railroads and factories closed, and the unemployed rioted. White House events were minimized, and the only public levee held was one on New Year's Day. Small, intimate dinners were given, but Van Buren was criticized for the extravagant menus. The President was said to be fond of ham, "washed down with champagne."

When Van Buren ran for reelection, Representative Ogle exaggerated the President's extravagant lifestyle in order to promote his candidate, William Henry Harrison. Ogle said, "How delightful it must be to a real genuine Locofoco to eat his Salade à la Volaille from a silver plate with a golden knife and fork." There were gold spoons at the White House, but they had been purchased earlier by James Monroe.

Peas, Green

Shell fresh peas—put in boiling water with 1 teaspoon salt and 1 teaspoon sugar and small bunch of mint. When peas are tender, remove mint and chop fine.

Put peas, mint and butter in bowl and mix.

Recipe from *The Cook's Own Book and Housekeeper's Register* by Eliza Leslie, 1835. ★

William Henry Harrison

№ 9

Harrison Cake

1 cup butter
2 cups molasses
3 to 4 cups flour
1 teaspoon ground cloves
1 teaspoon saleratus (baking soda)
1 cup sugar
1 cup sour cream
1 cup currants

Melt butter and stir into molasses. Sift flour, cloves and saleratus. Pour molasses mixture into dry ingredients and mix well. Add sugar and sour cream, and blend. Stir in currants and pour into cupcake molds. Bake at 375° F for 20–25 minutes. Yields 24 cupcakes.

Recipe adapted from *Godey's Lady's Book,* 1863. ★

The earliest known recipe for Harrison Cake appears in *The Young Housekeeper's Friend* by Mary Cornelius, 1850. It was not uncommon for a recipe to be named after a famous person. There are also cakes named after Washington, Jefferson, Madison, Lincoln and Hayes. Taft is the only President to have a pumpkin pie named after him. This recipe makes individual cupcakes, which may have been served at campaign parties.

Political campaigns have often enticed people to attend events by offering food and drink. In 1840, Harrison held a burgoo, or barbecue, in Wheeling, West Virginia. Thirty thousand people attended this rally. The amount of food consumed included 360 hams, 26 sheep, 20 calves, 1,500 pounds of beef, 8,000 pounds of bread, over 1,000 pounds of cheese, 4,500 pies and numerous barrels of hard cider. Harrison's campaign slogan was "Log Cabin and Hard Cider."

There were many inaugural balls given for President Harrison. One party in particular featured a pound cake in the shape of the U.S. Capitol. The cake was 6 feet tall, 9 feet wide and weighed 800 pounds.

General Harrison's Favorite Eggnog

4 eggs*
1 pint heavy cream
1½ quarts milk
½ pint bourbon
Sugar to taste
Nutmeg to garnish

Beat the eggs and fold into cream and milk. Add bourbon. Heat a little sugar in boiling water to make a syrup. Sweeten cream mixture with as much syrup as you like. Serve in a punch bowl with nutmeg sprinkled on top. ★

This is thought to be General Harrison's recipe for eggnog. Another version, called "Syllabub," can be found in *New Art of Cookery*, 1792. That recipe called for 2 cups of wine to be poured into a bowl, then placed underneath a cow. The cow was milked until the wine had "a fine froth at the top." (*Note: Consumption of raw eggs or milk is not recommended.)

☆ Baked Tomatoes

8 ripe tomatoes
Salt and pepper to taste
2 cups bread crumbs
4 tablespoons butter

Cut the tops off the tomatoes and scoop out the pulp from inside. Sprinkle cavities with salt and pepper. Finely chop the scooped-out pulp and mix with bread crumbs, 2 tablespoons melted butter, salt and pepper. Stuff into tomatoes and place in a baking dish. Dot tops with remaining butter. Bake at 350° F for 30–45 minutes or until tender. Serves 8. ★

Bird's Nest Pudding

If you wish to make what is called "bird's nest puddings," prepare your custard—take eight or ten pleasant apples, pare them, and dig out the core, but leave them whole, set them in a pudding dish, pour your custard over them, and bake them about thirty minutes.

Recipe from *The American Frugal Housewife*, "Dedicated to those who are not ashamed of economy," by Lydia Maria Child, 1844. ★

An Herb Sallad for the Tavern Bowl

Use all lettuces, sorrel, salad burnet, tarragon,
lovage, shallots, garlic, chives, chervil, watercress
and parsley

To make this condiment, your poet begs,
The powdered yellow of two hard-boiled eggs.
Two boiled potatoes passed through kitchen sieve,
Smoothness and softness to the salad give.
Let onion odours lurk within the bowl,
And half suspected animate the whole.
Of wondrous mustard add a single spoon.
Distrust the condiment that bites too soon.
But deem it not, thou man of herbs, a fault,
To add a double quantity of salt.
Fourtimes the spoon with oil of Lucca crown,
 And twice the vinegar procured from town.
Lastly o'er the flowery compound, toss
A magic soupspoon of Anchovy sauce.

Oh green and glorious, oh herbaceous treat.
T'wood tempt the dying authority to eat.
Backward to earth, he'd turn his weary soul,
And plunge his fingers in the sallad bowl,
Serenely full, the epicure would say,
"Fate cannot harm me—I have dined today!"
Sidney Smith, 1780

☆ Pork Chops with Spiced Apples

½ cup bread crumbs
½ cup flour
½ teaspoon fresh oregano
½ teaspoon fresh thyme
¼ teaspoon marjoram
Salt and pepper to taste
6 pork chops
2 tablespoons olive oil
1 cup uncooked rice
1 11-ounce can beef consommé
2 tart apples
1 tablespoon butter
1 tablespoon sugar
¼ teaspoon cinnamon

Mix together bread crumbs, flour and spices. Coat pork chops with flour mixture. Put oil in frying pan and brown pork chops on both sides. Remove from pan and keep warm. Add rice to pan and stir to coat with pan juices. Stir and cook until rice turns brown.

Slowly pour on consommé. Put chops back in pan. Cover and simmer for 20 minutes or until rice is done. Peel, core and slice apples. Melt butter in a separate saucepan. Sauté apples for 5 minutes, stirring occasionally. Mix in sugar and cinnamon. Arrange apples on plate with pork and rice. Serves 6. ★

President Harrison took great interest in the meals served at the White House and often did his own marketing to ensure that steaks or chops for his breakfast were good cuts of meat. He walked to the market in the early morning, wearing an old hat and carrying a market basket over his arm.

Once an assassin entered the White House, intending to kill Harrison. Fortunately two doormen caught the intruder, and the President himself cut a window cord and helped tie him up.

Harrison gave the longest inaugural speech of any President (1 hour and 45 minutes). He also had the shortest term of any President. He often went outside without a topcoat, gloves or hat. The President caught a cold that developed into pneumonia. He died only one month after taking the oath of office. His wife, Anna, had been sick at the time of the inauguration, so she stayed behind in Ohio. It was there that she received word of her husband's death. Although she was the wife of one President, and the grandmother of another (Benjamin Harrison), she never got to Washington.

"I wish that my husband's friends had left him where he is, happy and contented in retirement."

—*Anna Harrison*

John Tyler

"Tyler's Pudding"

4 eggs, slightly beaten
½ cup sugar
¼ teaspoon salt
1½ cups milk
¾ cup heavy cream
1 teaspoon vanilla extract
1 cup shredded coconut
1 unbaked 9-inch pie crust

Put eggs, sugar and salt in a bowl and beat until blended. Scald milk and cream in the top of a double boiler over hot water. Remove from heat and cool 5 minutes. Add 2 tablespoons of milk mixture to eggs and mix well. Pour egg mixture into milk, stirring constantly until blended. Add vanilla. Stir in coconut. Pour into pie crust. Bake at 450° F for 10 minutes. Reduce heat to 350° F and bake about 25 minutes or until done. Cool on a wire rack for 20 minutes, then refrigerate until ready to serve. ★

Tyler greatly enjoyed this pudding, which is more like a coconut custard pie.

Sally Lunn

1 package yeast
¼ cup warm water
½ cup butter
½ cup sugar
½ teaspoon salt
½ cup scalded milk
2½ cups flour
3 eggs

Mix yeast into warm water. Cream butter, sugar and salt. Stir in scalded milk. Add 2 cups of flour and mix well. Add eggs and yeast. Mix thoroughly. Stir in remaining flour and beat until smooth. Pour into a greased ring pan. Cover and let rise for 1 to 1½ hours, until doubled in size. Bake at 350° F for 35–45 minutes or until a straw inserted in the middle comes out clean. Serves 10. ★

There are many versions of this recipe. The bread was sold on the streets of London as "Soleil-Lune"—the sun and the moon. Sally Lunn, a woman who sold sweet buns in Bath, England, around 1790, is credited with creating the recipe.

Daniel Webster's Punch

24 lemons
2 pounds sugar (5⅓ cups)
1 cup green tea
1 quart brandy
3 quarts dry red wine
1 pint strawberries, sliced
1 orange, sliced
1 20-ounce can pineapple chunks
2 bottles champagne

Squeeze juice from the lemons, straining out all seeds and pulp. Add sugar, tea, brandy and red wine. Cover tightly and chill. Just before serving, pour into a punch bowl with ice, and add strawberries, orange and pineapple. Pour in champagne. Yields 2 gallons. *

This beverage was named after the statesman Daniel Webster. It was a popular drink at receptions.

Tyler was elected President on his fourth try. At that point his wife, Letitia, was in fragile health.

Her daughter-in-law Priscilla described Letitia as "... the most entirely unselfish person you can imagine. Not withstanding her very delicate health, Mother attends to and regulates all the household affairs and all so quietly that you can't tell when she does it."

Sadly, Letitia Tyler became the first wife of a President to die in the White House.

During the first part of Tyler's administration, Priscilla attended to the hostess duties. She was intelligent, beautiful and enjoyed meeting celebrities, including Daniel Webster.

At one State Dinner, Priscilla, who was pregnant with her second child, fainted and fell to the floor. Webster was close by and picked her up in his arms. Priscilla's husband, Robert, tried to revive her with a pitcher of water, but ended up dousing both his wife and Webster.

☆ How to Preserve a Husband

Be careful in your selection
Do not choose too young, and take only such
varieties as have been reared in a moral
atmosphere.

When once decided upon and selected, let that part
remain forever settled and give your entire
thought to preparation for domestic use.

Some insist on keeping them in a pickle,
while others are constantly getting them in hot water.

Even poor varieties may be made sweet, tender
and good
by garnishing them with patience, well-sweetened
with smiles and flavored with kisses.

Then wrap well in a mantle of charity. Keep warm
with steady fire of domestic devotion and milk of
human kindness.

When thus prepared, they will keep for a lifetime.
Author unknown

Some time after the death of Letitia, Tyler became infatuated with a lovely and flirtatious young woman from New York, Julia Gardiner. When they met, he was 53 and she was 23. Nicknamed the "Rose of Long Island", Julia had attracted the attention of many young men, including Tyler's son John Jr.

One day while on a boat trip with the President, there was an explosion on deck that killed Julia's father. Tyler was below deck enjoying champagne with Julia, and both were fortuitously unharmed. The accident brought the couple close together, and after Tyler proposed for the fourth time, Julia accepted. They were devoted to each other and she wrote this poem to him:

Let ruthless age then mark thy brow ...
It need not touch thy heart ...
And whate'er changes time may bring,
I'll love thee as thou art!

Tyler became the first President to marry while in office. He and Julia were secretly wed in New York. Their wedding supper included woodcock, pigeon, oysters and chicken salad. The next day, Tyler remembered the need to ratify the annexation of Texas. He said to his new wife, "Well, dear, we've ratified one treaty of immediate annexation at least without the advice and consent of the Senate."

☆ Chicken Salad

6 chicken breasts
4 peppercorns
4 whole cloves
1 bay leaf
1 teaspoon salt
1 teaspoon fresh thyme
1 bunch green grapes
6 hard-boiled eggs
1 cup olive oil
½ cup vinegar
Salt and pepper to taste
¾ cup pecans or almonds

Put chicken breasts in a large pot and fill with enough water to cover them. Add spices and simmer 20–30 minutes or until chicken is cooked. Remove chicken from pot. Let it cool. Remove and discard chicken skin. Cut the meat into cubes; place in a bowl. Cut grapes in half and add to chicken. Mash the egg yolks with oil. Add vinegar, salt and pepper; mix well. Chop egg whites and nuts; add to chicken. Stir in egg yolk mixture. Serves 10–12. ★

"Popularity, I have always thought, may aptly be compared to a coquette—the more you woo her, the more apt is she to elude your embrace."

—*John Tyler*

James K. Polk

№ 11

Polk took the presidency very seriously and considered himself hired to work. His wife, Sarah, was involved in his career and had political influence on him. She served as his campaign manager, personal secretary and official correspondent, and she scanned the newspapers to keep him informed of current events. She didn't enjoy retiring with the women after dinner, preferring to talk politics with the men instead. If a social event went on longer than it should, President and Mrs. Polk would stay up half the night to make up the lost work time.

When Polk ran for President, one woman said she was going to support Henry Clay because his wife had an excellent reputation as a housewife who made top-quality butter. Mrs. Polk replied, "If I should be so fortunate as to reach the White House, I expect to live on $25,000 a year, and I will neither keep house nor make butter." Some of the Polks' grocery lists survive, and they list butter as a frequent purchase.

Raspberry Shrub

4 cups fresh raspberries
1 teaspoon cider vinegar
Juice of 1 lemon
2 cups sugar
2 cups brandy

Place raspberries in a bowl and pour in vinegar and lemon juice. Add sugar and stir until dissolved. Crush the berries to a pulp with a spoon or potato masher. Cover the bowl with a cloth and let the mixture sit for 5 hours at room temperature.

Remove the cloth and strain the juice to remove all seeds and pulp. Mix brandy with the juice. Pour into sterilized jars and seal. This drink can be served at room temperature as an after-dinner drink, or served over crushed ice on a hot summer day.

Recipe adapted from *The American Frugal Housewife* by Lydia Maria Child, 1844. ★

President Polk occasionally sipped a Raspberry Shrub poured over crushed ice.

Scripture Cake

Original Recipe

½ cup Psalms 55:21
1 cup Jeremiah 6:20
1 tablespoon I Samuel 14:25
2 cups I Kings 4:22
II Chronicles 9:9 to taste
Pinch of Leviticus 2:13
2 teaspoons Amos 4:5
3 Isaiah 10:14
½ cup Judges 4:19
1 cup Numbers 17:8
1 cup I Samuel 30:12 (second food listed)
1 cup Nahum 3:12

Follow Solomon's advice for making a good boy, and you will have a good cake—Proverbs 23:14.

Updated Recipe

½ cup butter
1 cup sugar
1 tablespoon honey
2 cups flour
Spices (1 teaspoon cinnamon, ½ teaspoon nutmeg)
Pinch of salt
2 teaspoons baking powder

 3 eggs
½ cup milk
1 cup almonds, finely chopped
1 cup raisins
1 cup figs, chopped

Cream butter and sugar. Add honey. Sift flour, spices, salt and baking powder together and add to creamed mixture in thirds, alternating with eggs and milk. Beat until smooth. Stir in remaining ingredients. Grease and flour a Bundt pan or 9" x 5" loaf pan. Bake at 350° F for about 50 minutes or until done.

If desired, glaze the cake with a thin icing made of 1 cup powdered Jeremiah 6:20 (confectioners' sugar), 4 tablespoons hot Judges 4:19 (milk) and 1 teaspoon II Chronicles 9:9 (vanilla). Serves 12–15. ★

This is an old recipe, possibly Amish in origin. The recipe gives a quantity along with a Bible passage. The cook had to look up the verse in order to find out what ingredient is mentioned. There are many versions of the cake, some using different quantities and/or passages. The recipe can vary because some verses mention multiple foods or could be interpreted differently. For example, Judges 5:25 mentions water, milk and butter, and Jeremiah 6:20 mentions "sweet cane," which could be interpreted as molasses or sugar.

President and Mrs. Polk held very formal and solemn events while at the White House. They did away with serving food and drink at most receptions, and dancing was forbidden. Even at their inaugural balls, the dancing was stopped as soon as they arrived. The Polks stayed for a few hours and when they departed, dancing was resumed.

There were two inaugural balls. Tickets were $10 for the expensive ball, which featured a 4-foot-high cake that held a flag for each state and territory. It cost $2 to attend the other party, which ended up a free-for-all at the buffet table. At one reception, many guests had their hats, canes and cloaks stolen. One pickpocket got away with a wallet containing letters from former President Jackson and Dolley Madison.

Sarah Polk wore expensive Parisian gowns, and the public dressed regally to attend White House functions. One guest described a reception: "Milliners sent (the ladies) forth in fit trim to challenge the rainbow for the exquisiteness and variety of colors in which they were decked, while on their heads and bosoms glittering brilliants recline like nestling glowworms, darting forth rays of light in dazzling emulation."

Popovers

3 eggs, separated
1 cup flour
1 cup cream
1 tablespoon butter, melted
Salt to taste
½ cup Parmesan cheese

Blend egg yolks with flour, cream, butter and salt. Beat well. Fold in stiffly beaten egg whites. Grease muffin tins and fill half full. Sprinkle Parmesan cheese into each muffin cup. Add remaining batter. Bake at 450° F for 15 minutes. Reduce heat to 340° F and bake 20 minutes longer. Yields 12. ★

Popovers were a family favorite and served with many dinners. The Polks hosted the first formal Thanksgiving ever held in the White House. The event was so successful that it soon became customary.

The Polks rigidly observed the Sabbath and didn't accept social calls on Sundays. If a visitor happened to come by, Mrs. Polk would encourage the guests to attend church with them. Their Puritan ways also forbade all card playing.

During the Polk administration, social functions were sedate. The couple preferred plain dishes, but there was always an abundance of food. They hosted dinner parties up to three 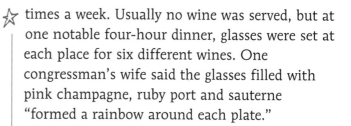 times a week. Usually no wine was served, but at one notable four-hour dinner, glasses were set at each place for six different wines. One congressman's wife said the glasses filled with pink champagne, ruby port and sauterne "formed a rainbow around each plate."

Bishop, Archbishop, or Pope

8 to 10 cloves
1 orange
½ lemon
2 tablespoons sugar
1 bottle port, claret or Burgundy
Ground nutmeg for garnish

This recipe has three different names, based on which type of wine is used: A Bishop is made with port, an Archbishop is made with claret and a Pope is made with Burgundy.

Stick cloves into the orange and put in a small baking pan. Roast at 350° F for 25–30 minutes. Cut into quarters and put in a medium-size saucepan. Add juice of ½ lemon and 3 or 4 strips of lemon peel. Add sugar and wine; simmer gently for 3–5 minutes. Pour into mugs and sprinkle with nutmeg. ★

Zachary Taylor

General Taylor served in the Northwest Territory, the Florida Everglades and Louisiana. While in Louisiana, he developed a love for Creole cooking, which he introduced to the White House. There are endless variations for making Jambalaya. Chicken, ham, sausage or fish can be substituted for the shrimp.

Taylor was nicknamed "Old Rough and Ready" because of his bravery in battle, but also because he frequently appeared in disheveled clothing.

One officer said, "He looks more like an old farmer going to market with eggs to sell ..." Another man said, "He wears an old oil cap, a dusty green coat and a frightful pair of trousers. On horseback he looks like a toad."

Taylor had been a frontier officer for most of his military career. His wife, Margaret, followed him to the many outposts to which he was assigned. Taylor praised her, saying, "My wife was as much a soldier as I was."

During the Mexican War, Mrs. Taylor took a vow that if her husband came home safely, she would never go into society again. She was 62 when her husband was elected President. Although she did entertain friends in her personal quarters, the hostess duties were taken over by their youngest daughter, Betty Bliss.

Jambalaya

¼ cup butter
2 cloves garlic, mashed
1 cup chopped tomato
1 red pepper, chopped
1 cup rice, uncooked
2½ cups chicken stock
2 cups shrimp, uncooked
½ cup olives
1 teaspoon Worcestershire sauce
1 teaspoon fresh thyme
¼ teaspoon cayenne pepper
Salt and pepper to taste

Melt butter in a large pan. Add garlic and sauté for 2 minutes. Add tomato and red pepper and sauté 3 minutes. Stir in rice until it is well coated with butter. Slowly add chicken stock. Add remaining ingredients. Cover and cook on low for 30 minutes or until rice is done. Serves 4–6. ★

Corn Fritters

½ cup flour
1 tablespoon sugar
1 tablespoon cornstarch
1 teaspoon baking powder
¼ teaspoon salt
1 egg, separated
⅓ cup milk
1 tablespoon olive oil
2 cups fresh corn (about 3 large ears)
1 tablespoon butter

Sift together dry ingredients. Lightly beat egg yolk. Stir yolk, milk and oil into the dry ingredients. Beat until smooth. Mix in corn. Beat egg white until stiff and fold into mixture. Melt butter in a skillet. Drop batter by spoonfuls into pan and cook over medium heat until brown. Flip and brown the other side. Serve with butter or maple syrup. Yields 6 fritters. *

Hominy Cheese Grits

1 cup grits, quick cooking
2 cups sharp cheddar cheese
2 cloves garlic, minced
½ cup butter
3 eggs
Pinch of salt

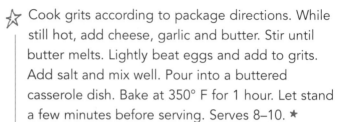

☆ Cook grits according to package directions. While still hot, add cheese, garlic and butter. Stir until butter melts. Lightly beat eggs and add to grits. Add salt and mix well. Pour into a buttered casserole dish. Bake at 350° F for 1 hour. Let stand a few minutes before serving. Serves 8–10. *

General Taylor loved hominy, but he was very particular that it be made from sweet corn. He discovered that his horse, "Claybank," was good at sniffing out the best bags of corn. Taylor would allow Claybank to wander among the Army provisions. When the horse gnawed a hole in a bag, Taylor would tell a private to remove the "contaminated" corn and mix up a batch of hominy.

Millard Fillmore

№ 13

Millard Fillmore was considered a very good-looking and well-built man. He was a natty dresser, and after being introduced to Queen Victoria, she declared him the handsomest man she had ever met.

Abigail Powers Fillmore was a bright and curious woman. She met her future husband when he was a student in her one-room schoolhouse. She was the first wife of a President to continue working after marriage.

Abigail was shocked to find that the White House had no library and didn't even have a copy of the Bible. After Congress appropriated $5,000, she purchased 800 books and created a library in the upstairs oval room.

The Fillmore administration was very austere and restrained. Dancing and alcohol were forbidden at White House parties, and the President and his wife preferred their food to be plain and simple.

Mrs. Fillmore attended dinners and receptions, but with a permanently injured ankle, it was torturous for her to stand in a receiving line. She relegated many duties to their daughter, Mary Abigail, who was named after her great-aunt, Abigail Adams.

Cauliflowers

To dress Cauliflowers: Having picked them into small pieces, which is absolutely necessary in order to remove the slugs with which this vegetable abounds, wash it thoroughly in several waters, and let it lay to soak for full an hour before you dress it. Put it in to a saucepan of boiling water, with a lump of salt, and when tender it will be done; let it drain in a colander, and serve it up with melted butter.

Some persons may prefer to see them brought to table whole, but they must then take the chance of being helped, along with the cauliflower, to some unsightly insect, which would be sufficient to disgust the least delicate stomach; besides, if properly boiled, and laid carefully in the dish, the pretty appearance of the vegetable is by no means destroyed by its having been divided.

Recipe from *The American Home Cook Book, with Several Hundred Excellent Recipes*, 1854. ★

Pot Roast

3 to 4 pounds round of beef
Salt and pepper to taste
1 ounce butter
1 chopped onion
2 cups bread crumbs
2 cups cold water
2 tablespoons flour
Watercress for garnish

Season the outside of the beef with salt and pepper. Combine the butter, onion, bread crumbs, salt and pepper to make a dressing. Cut incisions into the top half of the beef about 1 inch apart and fill these with the dressing. Put the meat in a pot with the water, and cover it tightly. Let simmer 4 hours or until meat is tender. When the meat is done, place it on a serving platter. Add flour to the pan juices and stir until it makes a smooth gravy. Let it boil once, and serve it in a gravy boat. Garnish with watercress. Serves 6–8. ✱

During Fillmore's term, the White House was updated, including installing the first bathtub with running water. Electric lights were put in, but both the President and his wife were so afraid of getting shocked that they wouldn't turn them on.

The White House also bought its first cast-iron stove around this time. It was a cause of great distress among the servants, who cooked in an open fireplace. The cook could not master the new "contraptshun."

Fillmore went to the Patent Office to learn how to work the stove. Here is a contemporary account: "The old black cook who had served many years at the White House was greatly upset when a range of small hotel size was brought to his quarters. He had managed to prepare a fine State Dinner for thirty-six people every Thursday in a huge fireplace, with the cranes, hooks, pots, pans, kettles and skillets; but he could not manage the draughts of the range, and it ended in a journey of the President to the Patent Office to inspect the model and restore peace in the kitchen."

Franklin Pierce

№ 14

Franklin Pierce was a handsome, successful and hard-drinking man. Following his inauguration, Pierce received visitors in the White House until past midnight. When he retired to his room, it was in such disarray that he had to search for a mattress to sleep on.

The most popular social events were the weekly concerts given by the Marine Band on the White House lawn. At one concert, a man approached Pierce and timidly asked if he might be allowed to tour the house. Pierce responded, "Why, my dear sir! That is not my house. It's the people's house. You shall certainly go through it if you wish." Pierce had a servant show the man around the mansion.

Pierce gave this impromptu toast on one Fourth of July:

"Life, lift the full goblet—away with all sorrow—
The circle of friendship what freedom would sever?
To-day is our own, and a fig for to-morrow—
Here's to the Fourth and our country forever."

Mrs. Pierce's Bird Seed Cookies

¾ cup butter
1½ cups brown sugar
2 eggs
1 teaspoon vanilla
1½ cups flour
¼ teaspoon baking powder
½ cup raw sesame seeds

Heat oven to 350° F. Cream butter with sugar. Add eggs and beat well. Add vanilla. Sift together flour and baking powder; add sesame seeds. Stir into creamed mixture. Drop by teaspoonfuls, 3 inches apart, onto greased baking sheets. Bake 10–12 minutes until lightly browned. Makes about 6 dozen.

Recipe provided by the Franklin Pierce Manse. It is thought to be an adaptation of one used by Jane Pierce. ★

Clam Soup Poem

First catch your clams—along the ebbing edges,
Of saline coves you'll find the little wedges,
With backs up, lurking in the sandy bottom;
Pull in your iron rake and lo! You've got 'em!
Take thirty large ones. Put a basin under,
And cleave, with knife their stony jaws asunder;
Add water (three quarts) to the native liquor,
Bring to a boil, and, by the way, the quicker
It boils the better, if you do it cutely.
Now add the clams chopped up and minced minutely,
Allow a longer boil of just three minutes,
And while it bubbles, quickly stir within its
Tumultuous depths where still the mollusks mutter,
Four tablespoons of flour and four of butter,
A pint of milk, some pepper to your notion,
And clams need salting although born of the ocean.
Remove from the fire; if much boiled they will suffer—
You'll find that a wood spoon is not much tougher.
After 'tis off add three fresh eggs, well beaten,
Stir once more, and 'tis ready to be eaten.
Fruit of the wave! O, dainty and delicious!
Food for the gods! Ambrosia for Apicius!
Worthy to thrill the soul of Venus,
Or titillate the palate of Silenus.

☆ A Dish of Snow

Grate the white part of cocoanut, put it in a glass dish and serve with currant or cranberry jellies.

Recipe from *Miss Beecher's Domestic Receipt Book* by Catharine Beecher, 1846. ★

You need not be from Pierce's home state of New Hampshire to enjoy a dish of snow. Catharine Beecher was from a prominent New England family. Her father and brother were clergymen, and her sister, Harriet Beecher Stowe, wrote *Uncle Tom's Cabin*.

Miss Beecher wrote *A Treatise on Domestic Economy* (1841). The purpose of her books was to make life easier for women and to elevate a woman's "sacred duties" to an academic level.

☆ James Buchanan

№ 15

James Buchanan was the only bachelor President. His niece, the beautiful and intelligent Harriet Lane, served as White House hostess. She often used fresh flowers in arrangements (before the mid-1800s, people thought it was unhealthy to bring fresh flowers indoors because they gave off harmful vapors).

Miss Lane was also given the delicate task of seating guests according to protocol, while keeping in mind any political feuds among the participants.

Buchanan was very particular about his food and had his butter sent to him from Philadelphia in a locked kettle. Harriet had a friend in Philadelphia who had become a political enemy of the President. She made copies of the kettle's keys and sent one to her friend. They corresponded "via the kettle" for years.

In 1860, Prince Albert of England became the first royal guest to ever stay at the White House. His traveling party was so large that Buchanan gave his bed to the Prince, and the President slept on a sofa in the hall.

The President and Miss Lane accompanied the Prince on a special trip to Mount Vernon to lay a wreath on George Washington's grave. The group traveled on the cutter ship *Harriet Lane* and enjoyed an elegant lunch catered by Gautier's of Washington. On the way back up the river, there was music and dancing aboard ship. This was quite a concession for the President, who considered dancing sinful.

Potatoes à la Duchesse

2 cups cold mashed potatoes
1 egg
½ teaspoon water

Take about ¼ cup of potatoes and form them into a flat cake or biscuit shape. Repeat until potatoes are used up. Arrange on a greased cookie sheet. Lightly beat egg. Add water to egg and mix. Brush egg wash over the tops of the potatoes. Bake at 400° F for 25–30 minutes, until golden. Yields 8 potato cakes. ★

Chestnut Flummery

1 15½-ounce can unsweetened chestnut purée*
2 cups milk
½ cup plus 2 tablespoons sugar
2 envelopes unflavored gelatin
4 tablespoons water
6 egg yolks
2 tablespoons dark rum or Grand Marnier
½ teaspoon vanilla
1 cup heavy cream

Blend chestnut purée and milk. Add sugar and mix in with a wire whisk. Soften gelatin in water for 5 minutes, then blend into chestnut mixture. Transfer to a saucepan and bring to a boil. Beat egg yolks. Gradually add a few tablespoons of the hot sauce to the yolks, stirring constantly. Then slowly pour egg yolk mixture into hot sauce, stirring constantly.

Cook about 5 minutes on low heat until thickened, but do not boil. Remove from heat; add rum and vanilla. Refrigerate for 1 hour. Whip cream and fold into mixture. Pour into a greased 2-quart mold and chill until firm, about 5 hours. Invert mold onto a platter. Serve with Chestnut Sauce.

*If chestnut purée is not available, you may substitute 15 ounces of canned chestnuts. Drain as much water as possible from chestnuts. Put them in blender or food processor and purée to a smooth paste.

☆ Chestnut Sauce

6 egg yolks
½ cup sugar
Pinch of salt
1 cup milk
1 cup heavy cream
1 teaspoon vanilla
5 ounces preserved chestnuts, chopped
¼ cup liquid from chestnuts

Beat egg yolks; mix in sugar and salt. Scald the milk and cream in the top of a double boiler over hot (not boiling) water. Very gradually add a few tablespoons of hot milk mixture to egg yolk mixture, stirring constantly. Return to double boiler and cook over hot water, stirring constantly, for 10 minutes or until thickened. Do not boil. Remove from heat and add remaining ingredients. Chill before serving. *

The term "flummery" comes from the Welsh word *llynru*. The dish was originally made with oatmeal, but by the late 17th century, cream or ground almonds were substituted. This updated version yields a sweet dessert resembling a firm pudding.

Sauerkraut

☆

2 pounds pork
2 tablespoons butter
2 large onions, chopped fine
1 tablespoon paprika
Salt to taste
1¼ cups water
2 pounds sauerkraut
1½ cups sour cream

Remove excess fat from pork and cut into cubes.
Set aside. Melt butter in frying pan. Sauté onions
until transparent. Add pork, paprika, salt and water
to pan. Simmer about 1½ hours, until pork is done.
Add drained sauerkraut to pan. If sauce is too thin,
sprinkle in a tablespoon of flour and stir. Add sour
cream just before serving. ★

Once a week, the President hosted elegant
State Dinners for 40 people. He enjoyed these
dinners for their dignified atmosphere and
sumptuous menus, but when he returned to
Wheatland, his Pennsylvania home, he preferred
simpler food such as mashed potatoes and
sauerkraut.

Buchanan had a legendary tolerance for
alcohol and once wrote to his liquor merchant,
reprimanding him for sending small bottles of
champagne. "Pints are very inconvenient in this
house, as the article is not used in such small
quantities," he wrote. On his way to church, he
liked to stop at the Jacob Baer distillery to
purchase a 10-gallon cask of "Old J.B." whiskey.
He found it amusing that he had the same
initials as the whiskey.

Scarborough Puffs

1 pint milk, scalded

1 cup flour

6 eggs

½ teaspoon salt

A scant tablespoon of butter

Lard or oil for deep frying

½ cup sugar

1 teaspoon cinnamon

Take 1 cup of scalded milk and slowly pour it into the flour, stirring until smooth. Add remaining milk and mix well. Cook this over medium heat until it is thick enough to hold a spoon upright. Remove from heat and cool 5 minutes. Beat eggs, then add to milk mixture, a bit at a time. Add salt and butter.

Put lard or oil in pan and heat 5–7 minutes on medium-high. Drop batter by tablespoonfuls into pan and cook like doughnuts until golden on both sides. Batter will puff up. Mix sugar and cinnamon in a bowl. Put puffs in bowl and coat with sugar mixture.

Recipe adapted from *Miss Beecher's Domestic Receipt Book* by Catharine Beecher, 1846. ★

 Buchanan never married, although he was briefly engaged to a woman named Anna Payne. He met a man named Rufus King, and the pair became virtually inseparable. They were sometimes referred to as "Miss Nancy and Aunt Fancy" or "Mr. Buchanan and his wife."

Parties were lavish affairs, and Miss Lane helped set a fashion trend by wearing "low necks and lace berthas." Mrs. Clement Clay of Alabama depicts the fashion of the time this way: "Jewels were conspicuous even in men's dressing, and gentlemen of fashion were rare who did not have varieties of sparkling studs and cravat-pins to add to the brightness of their vari-coloured [sic] vests…. President Buchanan was remarkable for his undeviating choice of pure white cravats."

Buchanan's four years in office were clouded by the approach of the Civil War. Buchanan did not seek a second term and was relieved to turn the office over to Abraham Lincoln. He said to Lincoln, "If you are as happy, dear sir, on entering this house as I am on leaving it and returning home, you are the happiest man in the country."

Abraham Lincoln

№ 16

Mrs. Lincoln's Courting Cake

1½ cups sugar
½ cup hot water
3 egg whites
½ cup butter
1½ cups flour
2 teaspoons baking powder
Dash of salt
1 teaspoon vanilla

Slowly heat ½ cup sugar in a heavy iron skillet, stirring continuously with a wooden spoon until the sugar becomes very dark brown. Slowly add hot water and stir until sugar dissolves. This is the caramelized syrup used in the cake. Beat egg whites until very stiff, and slowly add ½ cup sugar.

In another bowl, cream butter with remaining sugar. Sift together the flour, baking powder and salt, then add to the butter mixture, alternating with the syrup. Fold in egg whites. Flavor with vanilla and pour into two greased and floured 8" cake pans. Bake at 350° F for about 35 minutes. ★

This recipe is thought to be one that Mary Todd made for Lincoln when he was courting her. Abe tasted it and declared it, "... the best in Kentucky." Mary said of her husband, "Mr. Lincoln may not be a handsome figure, but people are perhaps not aware that his heart is as large as his arms are long."

Lincoln had the smallest appetite of any President. He often just nibbled at his food, and for dinner he sometimes ate only an apple, cheese and crackers. This frustrated Mary, who often planned elaborate meals, only to have her husband ask for a fruit salad.

Lincoln's law partner, Billy Herndon said, "Abe can sit and think longer without food than any man I ever met." However, Lincoln did have a sweet tooth, and one baker in Washington said the tall President was one of his best customers for pecan pie.

The menu for his inaugural lunch reflects his simple taste in food—Mock Turtle Soup, Corned Beef and Cabbage, Parsley Potatoes and Blackberry Pie were served. The centerpiece for the inaugural dinner was a model of the Capitol made from spun sugar.

Mrs. Lincoln's Frosting

½ cup butter
1 cup dark brown sugar
⅓ cup milk
2 cups powdered sugar

Melt butter in a heavy saucepan. Add brown sugar and cook over low heat for 2–3 minutes, stirring constantly while sugar melts. Remove from heat; slowly add milk and stir until smooth. Heat to just below boiling. Cool until lukewarm and gradually stir in powdered sugar. Beat vigorously until smooth. Use to frost a two-layer cake. Serves 10–12. ✱

As a young woman, Mary was vivacious and helped refine Lincoln's taste in clothes, manners and etiquette. She told her sister, "I do not think he knew pink from blue when I married him."

Lincoln disliked wearing formal clothes. They made him uncomfortable, and he constantly fidgeted with the kid gloves. He said shaking hands with a large group of people was "... harder work than splitting rails."

When they moved into the White House, Mrs. Lincoln thought it looked shabby, and one White House secretary said the mansion was like, "... an old and unsuccessful hotel." Mary put her energy into redecorating and had a grand levee to show off the house.

 Mrs. Lincoln was from the border state of Kentucky and was viewed with suspicion by Unionists. People from the South viewed her as a traitor, and she was constantly criticized from both sides. Members of Washington society boycotted the inaugural ball and several of her first receptions.

She compensated by spending large amounts of money on clothing and on redecorating the White House. Mrs. Lincoln's gown for the second inaugural ball cost $2,000. In one three-month period, she bought 100 pairs of gloves, some of which were never unwrapped. She overspent the decorating budget by $6,700 and put her family $29,000 in debt.

When the President found out about her overspending, he was furious and told her to stop buying "... flub dubs for this damned old house, when the soldiers cannot have blankets."

Mrs. Lincoln reveled in the fragrant flowers and exotic plants in the White House greenhouses and often sent bouquets to her friends. She enjoyed flower arranging and occasionally wore a circle of blossoms in her hair.

The Washington Star reported, "Through the good taste of Mrs. Lincoln, the stiff artificial flowers, heretofore ornamenting the presidential tables, were wholly discarded and their places delightfully supplied by fragrant, natural flowers."

Lincoln was the first President to bring his own small children to live in the White House. They helped relieve some of the tension of the war. Lincoln was a loving and somewhat indulgent parent, allowing the children to sell lemonade in a hallway crowded with job-seekers.

He loved to wrestle with his boys and let them pin down his arms and legs. They sometimes threw strawberries around at Cabinet meetings, and they'd climb on the furniture and scatter important papers.

His son Tad was slow to develop as a child. Historian Mathew Pinsker said that at age seven, "... he did not dress himself, nor could he read or write much until well into his teenage years."

This may be why Lincoln was particularly indulgent of Tad's escapades. The Secretary of War ordered a lieutenant's uniform made for the boy so he could play soldier. Tad then took his toy cannon and blasted the door during a Cabinet meeting. He once interrupted a formal tea party by riding through on a chair pulled by his pet goat, "Nanny."

"Nearly all men can stand adversity, but if you want to test a man's character, give him power."
—*Abraham Lincoln*

Union Pudding

Original Recipe

Take one cup of white sugar, three tablespoonfuls of flour, two eggs, one grated nutmeg, and one good-sized cocoanut grated fine, two teacupfuls of new milk and a tablespoonful of good fresh butter. Bake like tarts without an upper crust.

> Recipe from *Godey's Lady's Book*, 1865.

Updated Recipe

2 eggs
1 cup sugar
3 tablespoons flour
1 teaspoon grated nutmeg
1 tablespoon butter, melted
2 cups milk
½ to 1 cup grated coconut

Beat eggs lightly. Mix sugar, flour and nutmeg together. Add eggs and butter and blend. Add milk, a bit at a time, and mix well. Stir in coconut. Pour into individual ramekins. Place ramekins in a large baking dish; pour water into dish until it comes a third of the way up the sides of ramekins. Bake at 300° F for about 1½ hours or until a straw inserted in the middle comes out clean. *

 Godey's Lady's Book was a popular women's magazine published from 1830 to 1898. The magazine's popularity reached its zenith in the 1860s, when its circulation was 150,000.

Loyal Biscuits

3 cups flour, 1 cup sweet milk, 3 eggs, little sugar, butter the size of an egg, 3 spoonfuls baking powder. Bake as muffins.

> Recipe from the 1860s, *An Army Wife's Cookbook* by Alice K. Grierson. *

Quarreling Recipe

Take 1 root of sassafras and boil in 1 quart of water for 20–30 minutes. Put in a bottle and when your hubby comes home to quarrel, fill your mouth full and hold until he goes away. Granny said it was a "sure cure."

> Author unknown

Lincoln led the country through the bitter years of the Civil War. When he entertained friends, he tried to lighten the mood by telling witty stories, quoting poetry or reading aloud from Shakespeare.

He loved going to the theater, which he had never attended until being elected President. He was also a master of satire. After watching a lady with a feathered hat slip and fall, he quipped that she reminded him of a duck: "Feathers on her head and down on her behind." He said, "I laugh, because I must not cry; that is all—that is all."

Although the tradition of Thanksgiving began in Colonial days, Lincoln revived the custom during the war. In 1863, he declared the fourth Thursday of November as a day to thank God for His many blessings, and to remind people not of what had been lost, but of all that remained.

His son Tad, who had become very fond of one turkey, was upset to think that it would become Thanksgiving dinner. The President granted the turkey an official pardon, sparing its life. This tradition continues today.

Every Saturday the Marine Band played on the lawn of the White House. On occasion Lincoln made an appearance on the balcony, and he liked to lie on the sofa in the Blue Room and listen to the music. "Annie Laurie" was one of his favorite songs. The concerts were canceled after the death of the Lincolns' son Willie.

When news of Lee's surrender reached Washington, the city went wild with celebration. Three thousand people followed a brass band to the White House. Lincoln read his statement, then he had the Marine Band play "Dixie" and "Yankee Doodle Dandy" to symbolize that the states were once again united.

Lincoln's Log

(Jelly Roll)

¾ cup sugar
¾ cup flour
¾ teaspoon baking powder
Pinch of salt
4 eggs
1 teaspoon vanilla
¼ cup powdered sugar
½ to ¾ cup any flavor jelly

Sift together sugar, flour, baking powder and salt. Beat eggs lightly and mix in vanilla. Gradually add flour mixture to eggs and blend until smooth. Grease a 10" x 15" baking pan, then line with greased parchment paper. Pour batter into pan and smooth it out to the edges. Bake at 375° F for 12–14 minutes.

While cake is baking, cut an additional piece of parchment paper a little longer than your pan. Lay it on the counter and smear it with powdered sugar. Just before cake comes out, put jelly or jam in microwave for 30 seconds to soften it. When cake is taken from the oven, you must work quickly. Loosen the sides of the cake with a spatula. Place second sheet of parchment over top of the cake, then invert the pan onto the counter. Remove pan and peel paper off bottom of cake. Spread jelly or jam over the whole surface. While cake is still warm, roll it up from one side to the other. Place on plate with seam facing down. Dust with additional powdered sugar. ✳

Originally called jelly cakes, jelly rolls were made of several thin layers of cake with jelly spread between. The layers were stacked on top of each other and cut into wedges. In the 1880s, bakers began to make one long layer of cake, which was spread with jelly and then rolled up.

One of the early recipes for a jelly cake was published in *The American House Wife Cook Book*, by Miss T.S. Shute (1878). The recipe was from Laura Keene, a British actress who was performing in *Our American Cousin* at Ford's Theatre on the night Lincoln was shot. She was able to identify the assassin, John Wilkes Booth, who was a fellow actor. The jelly roll was sometimes referred to as Lincoln's Log.

After her husband was killed, Mary stayed upstairs for five weeks. Out of respect, President Johnson didn't move into the house until Mary was able to leave, so the public had almost unlimited access to the White House.

Mary Clemmer Ames wrote, "It was plundered not only of ornaments but of heavy articles of furniture. Costly sofas and chairs were cut ... Exquisite lace curtains were torn into rags and carried off in pieces."

Andrew Johnson

№ 17

Eliza Johnson's Sweet Potato Pudding

½ cup butter
4 cups grated raw sweet potato
½ cup sugar
1 cup raisins
1 teaspoon cinnamon
1 teaspoon allspice
½ teaspoon ground cloves
½ cup chopped nuts
1 cup molasses or corn syrup
3 eggs

Preheat oven to 325° F. Put butter in a heavy iron skillet and place in oven to heat up. Mix grated sweet potato with sugar, raisins, spices, nuts and molasses or corn syrup. Beat eggs lightly and mix into other ingredients. Pour this mixture into the hot skillet. Bake 10 minutes, then stir pudding. Repeat two more times to prevent a hard crust from forming. Bake a total of 30–40 minutes. Serve with Damson preserves or cream. Serves 8. ★

The Johnson family enjoyed being together and sometimes held popcorn parties. They preferred the country style cooking of Tennessee, and they liked to roast apples and chestnuts. When Johnson took over the presidency, his daughter Martha announced, "We are plain people from the mountains of Tennessee, called here for a short time by a national calamity. I trust too much will not be expected of us."

In spite of the criticism Johnson received during the impeachment proceedings, he was praised for his genial social skills. One journalist said, "The levees of President Johnson are especially brilliant, and frequenters of Washington society declare that under no former occupant of the White House has such good order and system reigned, as under the present."

Johnson took his family for picnics in nearby Rock Creek Park. His wife, Eliza, was frail and in poor health, so she attended only two White House functions—one was a party for the grandchildren and the other was the visit of Queen Emma of the Sandwich Islands, now called Hawaii.

Martha Johnson Patterson's Favorite Buckwheat Cakes

(President Johnson's Daughter)

In the evening mix:
1 quart buckwheat flour (4 cups)
4 tablespoons yeast
1 teaspoon salt
1 handful Indian meal (about ¼ cup)
2 tablespoons molasses (not syrup)
Warm water, enough to make a thin batter
  (about 5¼ cups)

Beat very well and set to rise in a warm place. If the batter is the least bit sour in the morning, stir in a very little soda, dissolved in hot water.

Mix in earthen crock and leave some in the bottom each morning—a cupful or so—to serve as a sponge for the next night instead of getting fresh yeast. In cold weather, this plan can be successfully pursued for a week or ten days without setting a new supply. Of course, you must add the usual quantity of flour, etc., every night and beat well. Do not make your cakes too small. Buckwheats should be of generous size. ★

Martha's granddaughter, Martha Willingham, talked of how Grandma Patterson made the buckwheat cakes: "She often remarked that it was a favorite of her father (President Johnson) and that she had taught the cooks in the White House to make it as he liked it."

An accomplished hostess, Martha undertook the renovation of the Executive Mansion. During the Civil War, the mansion had housed Union soldiers and was dowdy because of the overeager souvenir takers after Lincoln's death. Rats were even discovered in the East Room. Martha asked Congress to appropriate $30,000 for the mansion to be refurbished. She kept the house in good order, and on rainy days the velvet carpets were covered with muslin to keep off the mud.

Housekeeper's Alphabet

Apples—Keep in dry place, as cool as possible without freezing.

Broom—Hang in the cellar-way to keep soft and pliant.

Cranberries—Keep under water, in cellar; change water monthly.

Dish of hot water set in oven prevents cakes, etc., from scorching.

Economize time, health and means, and you will never beg.

Flour—Keep cool, dry and securely covered.

Glass—Clean with a quart of water mixed with tablespoon of ammonia.

Herbs—Gather when beginning to blossom; keep in paper sacks.

Ink Stains—Wet with spirits turpentine; after three hours, rub well.

Jars—To prevent, coax "husband" to buy our Cookbook.

Keep an account of all supplies, with cost and date when purchased.

Love lightens labor.

Money—Count carefully when you receive change.

Nutmeg—Prick with a pin, and if good, oil will run out.

Orange and Lemon Peel—Dry, pound and keep in corked bottles.

Parsnips—Keep in ground until spring.

Quicksilver and white of an egg destroys bedbugs.

Rice—Select large, with a clear, fresh look; old rice may have insects.

Sugar—For general family use, the granulated is best.

Tea—Equal parts of Japan and green are as good as English breakfast.

Use a cement made of ashes, salt and water for cracks in stove.

Variety is the best culinary spice.

Watch your backyard for dirt and bones.

Xantippe was a scold. Don't imitate her.

Youth is best preserved by a cheerful temper.

Zinc-lined sinks are better than wooden ones.

& regulate the clock by your husband's watch, and in all apportionments of time, remember the Giver.

From *Dixie Cook Book* by Estelle Woods Wilcox, 1883, owned by Martha Johnson Patterson, daughter of President Johnson.

Lancashire Pie

8 medium potatoes, peeled
½ cup butter
4 cups cubed beef (flank steak or roast)
Salt and pepper to taste
½ teaspoon savory
½ teaspoon sage
½ teaspoon thyme
½ to ¾ cup milk or cream

Cut peeled potatoes into quarters and boil a half hour or until soft. In large skillet, melt 4 tablespoons butter. Brown meat in butter and season with salt and pepper. Cook the meat slowly so it remains tender. Once potatoes are cooked, drain and place in a large bowl. Add remaining ingredients, plus more salt and pepper. Mash potatoes until smooth and creamy.

Grease a deep casserole dish. Place half of the meat in bottom, then put in half of the mashed potatoes and smooth them down. Layer the remaining meat over the potatoes and pour the juices from the skillet into casserole. Add the remaining potatoes on top. Smooth top of potatoes, then poke several holes and place a piece of butter in each hole. Bake at 350° F for 25 minutes or until golden brown on top. Serves 4–6. ★

Every morning Martha milked the cows, and then she made all the butter for the White House.

Andrew Johnson was a self-made man who grew up in extreme poverty. He taught himself to read, and when he married Eliza, she taught him math and writing. He had his own tailor shop by the time he was 17.

Even as President, he sometimes sewed his own clothes. At the end of the war, he returned to Tennessee "... to heal the breaches made by war." An old woman misunderstood and said, "Bless his dear heart, he's going to come back and open up a tailor shop."

Ulysses S. Grant

Mrs. Grant's Veal Olives

Original Recipe

Slice as large pieces as you can get from a leg of veal; make stuffing of grated bread, butter, a little onion, minced, salt, pepper, and spread over the slices. Beat an egg and put over the stuffing; roll each slice up tightly and tie with a thread; stick a few cloves in them, grate bread thickly over them after they are put in the skillet, with butter and onions chopped fine; when done, lay them on a dish. Make your gravy and pour over them. Take the threads off and garnish with eggs, boiled hard, and serve. To be cut in slices.

Recipe from *Our Own Cook Book*, by the Ladies of the First Presbyterian Church, Galena, Illinois, 1892.

Updated Recipe

1 leg of veal
3 cups bread crumbs
½ cup butter, softened
¼ cup chopped onion
Salt and pepper to taste
1 egg, beaten
A few whole cloves
1 tablespoon flour
¾ cup water
2 hard-boiled eggs, sliced

Slice large thin pieces of veal. Make stuffing with 2 cups of bread crumbs, ¼ cup butter, 2 tablespoons onion, salt and pepper. Spread this over the sliced veal. Brush beaten egg over the stuffing. Roll each slice up tightly; tie with kitchen string and stick in a few cloves. Sprinkle remaining bread crumbs over veal. Place in a skillet with remaining butter and onion and cook until lightly browned. Place on a platter. Stir flour into pan juices; blend in water and pour over the meat. Take the string off and cut into slices. Garnish with sliced eggs. Serves 8. ★

Grant's Lemon Pie

2 eggs
½ cup lemon juice
2 teaspoons grated lemon rind
1¼ cups sugar
¼ teaspoon salt
1 cup raisins
¼ cup water
⅓ cup shredded coconut
Pastry for two-crust 9-inch pie

Beat eggs lightly. Add all remaining ingredients except piecrust. Mix well. Line bottom of pie pan with half of the pastry dough. Pour filling into pan. Put top crust on pie and crimp edges together. Prick top crust in a decorative pattern. Bake 15 minutes at 450° F, then reduce heat to 300° F and bake an additional 20–25 minutes.

Recipe from *Margery Daw in the Kitchen* by Lucy Bostwick, 1887. (Several other versions of the recipe appeared in different cookbooks from New York State.) *

Mrs. Grant admitted that she couldn't cook, so there is some question as to whether these are her recipes.

In her memoirs she confesses, "Just before the Centennial Exposition, some ladies wanted to get up a cookbook and wrote to me for an original recipe. I did not know what to do. The cake I had obtained from a cookbook and the jelly I had considerable help with, and I was forced to ask the advice of a friend, who advised me to tell these ladies that I did not have an original recipe, did not know much about these matters and had always depended on my cook."

She may have not been able to cook, but Mrs. Grant had a flair for entertaining. Elegant dinners were prepared with the help of the White House chef.

The day of Grant's second inauguration was one of the coldest in inaugural history. The parade band had to stop playing because the condensation from their breath caused the instrument valves to freeze.

At the ball that night, 6,000 guests were expected, but only 3,000 attended. The building was so cold that guests wore their coats while dancing. Canaries had been brought in to add their voices to the dance music, but most of them froze in their cages.

A lavish feast had been laid out—roasted turkey, chicken, beef, ham, mutton, quail, partridges, lobster, salmon, scallops, oysters and stuffed boars' heads—but unfortunately, most of the food froze before it could be eaten. The guests drank hot cocoa and coffee instead of champagne, and many left early.

Julia Grant took great interest in social affairs, but General Grant disliked following the rules of etiquette. After finishing the required dancing at one party, he confided to a friend, "I'd rather storm a fort!"

Mrs. Grant thoroughly enjoyed her role as First Lady. She said, "... Life at the White House was a garden spot of orchids, it was a constant feast of cleverness and wit, a co-mingling with men who were the brainiest their states and countries could send to represent them, and women unrivaled anywhere for beauty, talent and tact. When Congress and society get in session, Washington is a mecca for brains and beauty."

☆ Cucumber Salad

Original Recipe

Let them be as fresh as possible, or they will be unwholesome. Pare: cut off the stem end to the seeds, and slice in cold water, some time before they are wanted. Serve with salt, pepper, vinegar; and if you like a little salad oil. Onions are sometimes sliced up with them—and tomatoes are frequently prepared in the above manner.

Recipe from *The American Home Cook Book* by an American Lady, 1854.

Updated Recipe

3 medium cucumbers
½ cup cider vinegar
¼ cup olive oil
1 tablespoon sugar
Salt and pepper to taste

Peel cucumbers and slice them in rounds. Discard end pieces. Make a dressing of the remaining ingredients and pour over cucumbers. Stir to coat well. Serves 4–6. ★

Grant was very fond of cucumbers. He could make a meal of a sliced cucumber and coffee.

Roman Punch

1 quart lemon sherbet
1 cup rum
¼ cup Cointreau
1 split of champagne

Put lemon sherbet into a chilled bowl. Slowly mix in rum and Cointreau. Quickly add champagne and stir until it is a mushy texture. Ladle into sherbet dishes. Serves 10. ★

Grant originally brought his Army quartermaster to serve as the White House cook. The food was basic and unimaginative. Turkey was frequently served as the fancy meal. When large important State Dinners were held, the cook simply prepared a bigger turkey.

Mrs. Grant rebelled and hired an Italian chef named Melah. After that, State Dinners became extravagant affairs, which sometimes lasted up to three hours and included 29 courses with six separate wines. Roman Punch was served after the entrée to give guests time to digest their dinner.

This punch was also served at the wedding of the Grants' daughter, Nellie. Grant was not pleased when she fell in love with an Englishman, but he hosted an opulent wedding nonetheless.

Mrs. Grant had thousands of fragrant flowers placed in the White House, and garlands of

 roses hung from the chandeliers. The bride wore a $5,000 gown, and the dinner held in the State Dining Room featured menus printed on satin.

Nellie was the President's only daughter, and when the couple left for England, Grant was found in her room, sobbing uncontrollably.

Nellie Grant's Wedding Breakfast
May 21, 1874

Soft Crabs on Toast
Gateaus garnis de Crabes et Champignons
Sauce à la Crème
Croquettes of Chicken with Green Peas
Cotelettes d'Agneaut   Sauce à la Tartare
Aspic de langues de Boeuf à la Moderne
Woodcocks and Snipes on Toast
Broiled Spring Chicken
Salade Sauce Maillenaise   Bride's Cake
Strawberries with Cream
Charlotte Russe   Broques en Bouche
Corbeils glaces à la Jardiniere
Gateaux de Trois Freres
Epigraphe la fleur de Nelly Grant
Pudding à la Nesselrode Sauce à Gelee
Blamangea la Napoleon
Plombieres garnis de Fruits à Fleures Glaces
Ice Cream   Water Ices
Small Cakes   Punch à la Romaine
Coffee   Chocolate

Rutherford B. Hayes

№ 19

Rutherford B. Hayes was a good-natured man who liked to wear comfortable clothes, no matter how poorly they fit. His wife, Lucy, was popular and well-liked.

She had a good sense of humor and was described as cheerful, calm and serene. One newspaperman wrote, "Her beauty and simplicity have taken blasé Washington by storm." Longfellow, Holmes and Whittier all dedicated poems to her.

Mrs. Hayes was the first wife of a President to be called "First Lady" and was the first with a college degree. She was involved in the suffrage movement, Civil Service reform and reconstruction of the South.

She also took great interest in political affairs and often advised her husband. A member of the press jokingly said, "In the absence of his wife, Mr. Hayes is acting President."

French Pickles

1 peck green tomatoes
6 large onions sliced

1 tea cup full (4–6 ounces) of salt-thrown on them—Stand till morning—drain them thoroughly—then boil in 2 quarts water, a (one? Torn) quart vinegar 15 or 20 minutes—then strain in a collender (colander)—take 4 quarts vinegar, 2 lbs brown sugar, ½ lb white mustard seed, 2 table spoons full grown allspice x 2 of cloves, & 2 of cinnamon, 2 of ginger, 2 ground mustard, thrown together & boil 15 minutes—Excellent.

9 October 1873. (from) Mrs. (Maria) Vallette (Fremont, Ohio)

Recipe handwritten by President Hayes in a family cookbook. Supplied by the Rutherford B. Hayes Presidential Center. ★

Mrs. Hayes' Corn Bread

Original Recipe

2 pints Meal
1 pint Jar Milk with 1 teaspoon Soda
1 egg well beaten, mixed with cornmeal
A little pinch of salt

Add a little more milk if needed. Have the pan well buttered and very hot.

Updated Recipe

3 tablespoons butter
3 cups stone-ground cornmeal
1 cup flour
2 tablespoons brown sugar
2 teaspoons baking powder
1 teaspoon baking soda
½ teaspoon salt
1 egg
2 cups milk

Preheat oven to 425° F. Melt butter in a heavy iron skillet. Put dry ingredients in a large bowl and mix. Lightly beat egg in a small bowl and pour in milk. Pour into dry ingredients and stir until just blended. Add more milk if mixture is too dry. Quickly pour into hot skillet. Bake for 25–30 minutes or until a straw inserted in the middle comes out clean. Serve hot from oven. Yields about 10 servings.

Original corn bread recipe, believed to be in Mrs. Hayes handwriting, was found on a folded piece of paper in the back of one of her cookbooks, *Practical Cooking and Dinner Giving*, 1878. Recipe supplied by the Rutherford B. Hayes Presidential Center. ★

President and Mrs. Hayes entertained in an opulent fashion and spent $3,000 on one reception alone. The mansion was often full of overnight guests, and young Rutherford Hayes once quipped that when he visited, he felt lucky to get, "... the soft side of the billiard table."

The First Lady employed the first full-time flower arranger for the White House, and instead of paying visits to all the diplomatic wives, she sent bouquets of flowers with a card explaining how to care for the flowers.

The couple treated the staff fairly, and Colonel Crook, the White House Disbursing Officer, said he never heard any employee reprimanded. All of the secretaries, clerks and their families were invited to join the First Family for a turkey dinner every Thanksgiving, and all staff members received a Christmas present.

Lemonade Lucy's Lemonade

Original Recipe

Rub loaf-sugar over the peels of the lemons to absorb the oil; add to the lemon-juice the sugar to taste. Two lemons will make 3 glassfuls of lemonade, the remainder of the ingredients being water and plenty of ice chopped fine.

Recipe from *Practical Cooking and Dinner Giving* by Mary F. Henderson, 1878.

Updated Recipe

2 lemons
⅓ cup sugar
⅓ cup water
Crushed ice

Grate the rind of both lemons, using the smallest holes available. Mix the lemon peel into the sugar, and allow it to sit for about 20 minutes, so that the sugar will absorb the lemon oil. Squeeze juice from lemons and add sugar, stirring until dissolved. Pour juice into pitcher and add water. Stir and adjust sweetness if desired. Fill three tall glasses with crushed ice and add lemonade. Serves 3. ✱

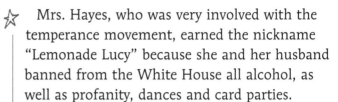

Mrs. Hayes, who was very involved with the temperance movement, earned the nickname "Lemonade Lucy" because she and her husband banned from the White House all alcohol, as well as profanity, dances and card parties.

When the President's niece, Emily Platt, married General Russell Hastings in the Blue Room, the White House was lavishly decorated ... and after the ceremony, the couple was toasted with coffee, tea and lemonade.

Following one dinner, Secretary of State William M. Evarts commented, "It was a brilliant affair; the water flowed like champagne."

The most popular dish served at the White House was the fruit platter. The oranges were especially well liked, since the staff surreptitiously filled them with Roman Punch, a frozen drink containing strong rum. The platters were referred to as "The Life-Saving Station."

Hayes was the one who got the last laugh, though. He said, "The joke of the Roman Punch was not on us, but on the drinking people. My orders were to flavor them rather strongly with the same flavor that is found in Jamaican rum. There was not a drop of spirits in them."

Oyster Stew

1 quart oysters
½ pint cream
Salt to taste
Cayenne pepper to taste
3 tablespoons butter

Put a quart of oysters on the fire in their own liquor. The moment they begin to boil, skim them out, and add to the liquor a half-pint of hot cream, salt and cayenne pepper to taste. Skim it well, take off the fire, add to the oysters an ounce and a half of butter broken into small pieces. Serve immediately.

Recipe from *Practical Cooking and Dinner Giving* by Mary F. Henderson, 1878. ★

Hayes enjoyed oysters prepared in many ways. They were served often in the White House and at Spiegel Grove, the family's home in Ohio.

The President and First Lady celebrated their silver wedding anniversary with a two-day jubilation party, which included a reenactment of the ceremony and the baptism of two grandchildren. Mrs. Hayes wore her wedding gown of white silk and brocade.

Dolley Madison had initiated the tradition of rolling Easter eggs on the lawn of the Capitol. Children gathered on Easter Monday and held contests to see which eggs could reach the bottom of the sloping lawn without being broken by the competitors. When members of Congress complained that broken eggshells were ruining the grass, a bill was enacted banning egg rolling on the Capitol grounds.

Mrs. Hayes loved children and revived the tradition by inviting boys and girls from Washington to roll their Easter eggs on the White House lawn.

James A. Garfield

№ 20

Mrs. Garfield's White Loaf Bread

1 yeast cake, crumbled
1 cup hot water
2 tablespoons sugar
1½ tablespoons unsalted butter
2½ teaspoons salt
1 cup scalded milk
6½ cups bread flour
2 tablespoons melted butter

Crumble yeast cake into ½ cup hot water. Add 1 tablespoon of sugar and stir until dissolved. Put butter in a mixing bowl; stir in salt, milk and remaining hot water and sugar. Cool to lukewarm (85° F). Blend in yeast mixture. Sift in half of the flour, beating well. Mix remaining flour in by hand. Place dough on a lightly floured pastry board. Cover with a cloth and let stand for 10–15 minutes.

Knead dough for about 10 minutes, until it becomes smooth and no longer sticks to the board. Place dough in a greased bowl, and turn it over several times to coat with the grease. Cover with a damp cloth and put in a warm place. Let rise about 2 hours, until doubled in size.

Punch dough down and knead again. Put back on the pastry board and divide into two equal portions. Cover with a cloth for 10 minutes. Grease and flour two 5" x 9" heavy bread pans. Shape the loaves and put them into the pans. Cover with a damp cloth and let them rise again, until almost doubled in bulk.

Bake at 450° F for 10 minutes. Reduce heat to 350° F and bake for 30 minutes longer. The bread is done when it shrinks from sides of pan. Brush the tops with melted butter, then return loaves to the oven for a few more minutes. Cool in pans for a few minutes before putting on a rack. Yields 2 loaves. ★

President Garfield and his wife, Lucretia, shared a love of literature and cultural events, and they belonged to the Literary Society of Washington. Mrs. Garfield found household chores to be mundane. Her positive philosophy of life overcame the boredom of bread baking by varying the shape and size of the loaves.

She later wrote, "The very sunshine seemed to be flowing down through my spirit into the white loaves, and now I believe ... that I need not be the shrinking slave of toil, but its regal master."

The Garfields had five children. The two younger boys sometimes held bicycle races in the East Room. Mealtimes for the family were a period of instruction for the children. Garfield considered his house—including the White House—to be a "place for plain living and high thinking."

"His table was bountifully supplied with plain well-cooked food, but he made his meals such feasts of reason that his guests scarcely noticed what they ate," reported *The Century Magazine* about dinner with the Garfields.

☆ 'Cold' Slaw

2 egg yolks
1 cup cream
4 tablespoons vinegar
3 tablespoons butter
2 tablespoons sugar
1 tablespoon mustard
1 teaspoon celery seed
Salt and pepper to taste
1 head cabbage

Beat egg yolks lightly and put in a small pan. Add all remaining ingredients except cabbage. Heat until mixture just begins to boil, stirring constantly. Finely chop cabbage and place in a bowl. Stir in hot dressing. Chill before serving.

Recipe adapted from *The Presbyterian Cook Book*, Dayton, Ohio, 1873. ✶

"What a terrible responsibility to come to him—and to me."

—*Lucretia Garfield*

Rissables

Original Recipe

Rissables are made with veal and ham chopped very fine, or pounded lightly; add a few bread crumbs, salt and pepper, nutmeg and a little parsley and lemon-peel; mix all together with the yelks [sic] of eggs, well beaten; either roll them into shape like a flat sausage or into the shape of a pear, sticking a bit of horseradish in the ends to resemble the stalk. Egg each over (dip in beaten egg) and grate bread crumbs (roll in bread crumbs); fry them brown, and serve on crisply fried parsley.

Recipe from *Godey's Lady's Book*, 1868.

Updated Recipe

1 pound ham, ground
1 pound veal, ground
⅓ cup bread crumbs
2 eggs
1 tablespoon Worcestershire sauce
1 tablespoon parsley
1 teaspoon grated lemon peel
1 teaspoon nutmeg
Salt and pepper to taste
¼ cup corn oil

Mix together all ingredients except corn oil, and shape into 2-inch-diameter patties. Heat oil in a fry pan. Fry meat patties over medium-high heat until golden brown and cooked through. Flip patties to ensure even cooking. Serves 8–10. ★

The name "Rissables" comes from the French verb *rissoler*, which means "to brown."

After Garfield's inauguration, a large reception was held in the National Building Museum in Washington, D.C. There were so many guests that they were served 500 at a time. Food for the event included 1,500 pounds of turkey, 200 gallons of chicken salad, 700 loaves of bread, 2,000 biscuits, 150 gallons of ice cream and 15,000 cakes.

Soon after taking the oath of office, Garfield was besieged by people seeking jobs. One contemporary account said, "They stopped his carriage in the street; they called him out of bed; they bored him in the railroad carriages and stations ... they covered him with flattery more contemptible than slander ..."

Garfield was annoyed that so much of his time was taken up with these matters. He said, "I have been dealing all these years with ideas ... I have been heretofore treating of the fundamental principles of government, and here I am considering all day whether A or B should be appointed to this or that office. My God! What is there in this place that a man should ever want to get into it?"

Garfield was one of the most intellectual Presidents. He taught Greek and Latin at Hiram College, later becoming its president. He was elected to the House of Representatives and then to the Senate. Garfield was the first left-handed President ... he sometimes showed off by writing Greek with one hand and Latin with the other.

By the time he became President, the Garfields were familiar with the demands of Washington. They gave receptions and held a few formal dinners. According to one visitor, "He (Garfield) was well-dressed, of splendid figure, his dome-like head erect, adequately supported by immense shoulders, and he looked the President indeed ... It was a supreme hour—and only an hour."

On July 2, 1881, the President was en route to his college reunion when he was shot by a disappointed office seeker. He lingered in agony for two months and died on September 19.

The assassin, Charles Guiteau, had purchased a gun and visited the local prison to see what it would be like to be incarcerated. After shooting Garfield, Guiteau was arrested, and from his prison cell, he wrote the new President, Chester Arthur. "My inspiration is a godsend to you ... It raised you from a political cipher to the president of the United States."

Chester A. Arthur

№ 21

President Arthur was a stylish man who loved good food and fancy clothes. He was nicknamed "Elegant Arthur" because he changed clothes for every occasion in the day. It was reported that he had 80 pairs of pants.

When he traveled, Arthur brought along his own chef. If he rode on the presidential railroad car, he brought his own wine, china, silver and linens. Arthur felt entitled to live a life of luxury.

Dinners at the White House were elegant, and Arthur could be a charming host. John S. Wise considered him "a very prince of hospitality," but one woman portrayed him as being "quite like a gigantic icicle." And his enemies called him "The Dude."

Arthur was a widower when he became President. His sister, Mary McElroy, often performed hostess duties, but Arthur never allowed anyone to permanently assume the position that should have belonged to his wife.

Spiced Nuts

1½ cups sugar
1 teaspoon cinnamon
3 tablespoons water
1 cup pecans or almonds

Mix ½ cup of sugar and cinnamon in a small bowl and set aside. Put remaining sugar in a small pan and add water. Boil for 5 minutes on medium-low heat. Add nuts and stir to coat well with sugar. Working quickly, lift nuts by spoonfuls into dry sugar mixture and roll until well coated. Separate nuts and cool on a hard surface. Store in an airtight container. Yields 1 cup. ✴

According to Arthur, the White House looked like a "badly kept barracks," and he refused to move in until renovations were made. He argued with Congress over the necessary repairs, finally declaring, "I will not live in a house looking this way. If Congress does not make an appropriation, I will go ahead and have it done and pay for it out of my own pocket. I will not live in a house like this."

Congress did provide some funds, and Arthur proceeded to hire Louis Comfort Tiffany, a New York decorator. The White House was cleared of unwanted items, and 24 wagonloads of "claptrap" were carted off and sold at public auction. The new decor featured plush velvet fabrics, gold wallpaper and a silver ceiling, plus a large glass screen erected in the front hall. Arthur was fastidious and supervised every detail of the renovations.

"I may be President of the United States, but my private life is nobody's damned business."

—*Chester Arthur*

☆ Asparagus with Eggs

1 bunch asparagus
Salt and pepper to taste
3 tablespoons butter, melted
4 eggs
2 tablespoons cream
2 tablespoons lemon juice

Wash and dry the asparagus. Cut off the tough ends and discard. Place asparagus in the bottom of a 9" x 9" baking pan. Season with salt and pepper and pour 2 tablespoons melted butter on top. Beat eggs to a froth. Add cream, lemon juice, remaining butter and more salt and pepper. Mix well and pour over asparagus. Bake at 350° F for 20–25 minutes. Serves 6. ✳

Mulligatawny Soup

¼ cup butter
1½ tablespoons flour
1 tablespoon curry powder
2 cloves garlic
½ cup diced onion
1 celery stalk, diced
1 carrot, peeled and diced
5 cups chicken broth
1 cup cooked rice
1 cup diced cooked chicken
½ cup diced tart apple
¼ cup lime juice
¼ teaspoon thyme
Salt and pepper to taste
½ cup coconut milk

Melt butter in a large pot. Blend in flour and curry powder and cook 3 minutes. Add garlic, onion, celery and carrot. Sauté 5 minutes. Slowly add chicken broth and stir until smooth. Add all remaining ingredients except coconut milk. Cover and simmer 30 minutes. Just before serving, stir in coconut milk. Makes about 8 cups. ★

President Arthur stayed up very late, often working or socializing until 2 or 3 a.m. He and his society friends drank lavish amounts of champagne and imported wine, and they feasted on pheasant, mussels, sweetbreads and other delicacies. He also enjoyed giving tours of the White House in the middle of the night.

Punctuality was not one of Arthur's strong points. He often arrived late for meetings, but he carried a basket of official-looking papers to give the impression that he'd been hard at work. One official said, "President Arthur never did today what he could put off until tomorrow."

"Nobody ever left the Presidency with less regrets, less disappointment, fewer heartburnings, nor more general content with the result of his term (in his own heart, I mean) than I do."
—*Chester Arthur*

Bass with Caper Sauce ☆

1 3- to 4-pound bass
2 slices bacon
¼ cup chopped onion
1 cup chopped mushrooms
1 teaspoon sage
Salt and pepper to taste
1 cup bread crumbs
½ lemon
3 tablespoons flour
1¼ cups chicken broth
½ cup cream
2 tablespoons capers

Clean fish and remove head and bones. Put bacon into a pan and cook until crispy. Remove bacon and crumble. Add onion to bacon fat and sauté until translucent. Add mushrooms, sage, salt and pepper. Sauté 3–4 minutes. Remove from pan and mix with bread crumbs and bacon. Loosely stuff mixture into fish; close opening with skewers or kitchen string. Place in a baking dish. Squeeze lemon over fish. Bake at 400° F for 30–40 minutes.

Pour off all but 3 tablespoons bacon fat. Add flour and blend; cook 2 minutes. Gradually stir in broth; cook until thickened. Add cream, capers, salt and pepper. Pour over fish. Serves 6. ★

In his day, President Arthur was one of the best fishermen in America. He once caught an 80-pound bass off the coast of Rhode Island. He also enjoyed this sport because it got him out of Washington.

Arthur unofficially began the custom of the continental breakfast. He ate a roll and drank his coffee while getting dressed. His lunch never featured meat, but his favorite dinner was mutton chops and a glass of beer.

Grover Cleveland

№ 22 & 24

G rover Cleveland was a 48-year-old bachelor when he became President. His sister Rose performed hostess duties for his first year in office. Rose was an intellectual woman, and if a receiving line became too tedious, she would silently conjugate Greek verbs to keep from getting bored.

Rose also acted as chaperone during the President's secret courtship of young Frances "Frank" Folsom. Miss Folsom was the daughter of Cleveland's law partner; after her father died, she became Cleveland's ward. Cleveland was a devoted guardian who oversaw her education and spent a great deal of time with Miss Folsom and her mother.

Cleveland is the only President to be married in the White House. His bride was none other than his former ward, 22-year-old Frances, the youngest First Lady ever. The President wrote out the invitations himself and supervised every detail of the wedding. John Philip Sousa led the Marine Band. As they started to play Mendelssohn's "Wedding March," the President slowly descended the staircase with Miss Folsom on his arm.

A simple ceremony took place in the Blue Room. Garlands of roses hung from the doors, and the couple's initials were spelled out in roses on the mantel. Scarlet begonias were placed in the fireplace to resemble flames. The wedding supper featured terrapin, breast of spring chicken, cold meats, salads, fish, pâté de foie gras, ice cream molds, bonbons and fruits.

Cleveland enjoyed good food and was nicknamed "Uncle Jumbo" because he weighed 250 pounds. He never liked French food, though, and the French chef from the Arthur administration had remained at the White House.

The President once wrote, "I must go to dinner. I wish it was to eat a pickled herring, Swiss cheese and a chop at Louis' instead of the French stuff I shall find." Cleveland eventually hired a cook named Eliza, who prepared the plainer food that he preferred.

Cleveland occasionally played poker on Sundays. He said, "My father used to say that it was wicked to go fishing on Sundays, but he never said anything about draw-poker."

Maids of Honor

Original Recipe

Take one cupful of sour milk, one of sweet milk, a tablespoonful of melted butter, the yolk of four eggs, juice and rind of one lemon, and small cupful of white pounded sugar. Put both kinds of milk together in a vessel, which is set in another, and let it become sufficiently heated to set the curd, then strain off the milk, rub the curd through a strainer, add butter to the curd, the sugar, well-beaten eggs, and lemon. Line the little pans with the richest of puff-paste, and fill with the mixture; bake until firm in the center, from ten to fifteen minutes.

Recipe from *The White House Cook Book* by Mrs. F.L. Gillette and Hugo Ziemann, 1887.

Updated Recipe

Filling
2 lemons
3 tablespoons flour
¾ cup powdered sugar
1½ cups buttermilk
2 tablespoons butter
3 eggs
1 teaspoon lemon zest
1 teaspoon vanilla

 Crust
1 cup graham crackers, crushed
¼ cup sugar
5 tablespoons butter, melted
1 teaspoon lemon zest

Squeeze lemons and set juice aside. Combine flour and powdered sugar in a saucepan. Slowly add buttermilk, stirring to avoid lumps. Cook over medium heat, stirring occasionally, until mixture thickens. Stir in butter. Beat eggs lightly and mix with lemon juice and zest. Mix into pan and cook for an additional 5–7 minutes, until thick. Remove from heat and add vanilla.

Combine crust ingredients. Put about 2 tablespoons in the bottom of individual dessert cups; press down to form bottom crust. Pour filling on top and sprinkle with any remaining crumbs. Chill 2 hours. Serves 8.

Recipe adapted from *The White House Cook Book* by Mrs. F.L. Gillette and Hugo Ziemann, 1887. ★

"The Ship of Democracy, which has weathered all storms, may sink through the mutiny of those on board."

—*Grover Cleveland*

Mrs. Cleveland was immensely popular. She hosted afternoon receptions each week, and for the first time, they were held on Saturday so working women could attend. The events became so popular that the waiting line to get in stretched from the White House to the Treasury Building. At one reception, the First Lady shook 9,000 hands. She had to take short breaks to have her arm massaged.

Mrs. Cleveland never drank wine, while her husband was a connoisseur. Seven or eight wine glasses were put at each place for State Dinners. He disliked receptions and entertained only when it was absolutely necessary.

Souvenirs were often given to dinner guests. The ladies received a ribbon with their name and the date—one end featured a picture of the White House while the other side had the United States coat of arms. The men were given a smaller ribbon with their name, date and the coat of arms.

After a four-year term in office, Cleveland lost his bid for reelection. Mrs. Cleveland was especially disappointed, but she told the White House staff to keep everything in order for when they returned. Her prediction came true—four years later, Cleveland was reelected, making him the only President to serve nonconsecutive terms in office.

When they returned to the White House, the Clevelands brought with them a 1-year-old daughter, Ruth (for whom the Baby Ruth candy bar was named). When Frances gave birth, reportedly half of the women in America knitted booties for the baby. The grounds of the White House were open to the public, and people often came up to the baby carriage to see the little girl. Sometimes strangers picked her up, and after one person tossed Ruth in the air, the grounds were closed to the public.

Brown Bread

1 cup cornmeal
1 cup rye flour
1 cup whole wheat flour
2 teaspoons baking soda
1 teaspoon salt
1 cup buttermilk
¾ cup molasses

Sift dry ingredients together. Stir in buttermilk and molasses. Beat well. Pour into bread pan, filling two-thirds full. Wrap waxed paper over top and sides; tie securely around the pan. Place a trivet in the bottom of a large pot and put in about an inch of water. Get the water boiling, then put the bread pan on the trivet, so that the water is not touching the pan.

Cover the pot and let bread steam for 2½ hours. Add water to pot occasionally so it won't boil dry. Remove bread from pot and take off paper. Bake bread in 350° F oven for 20 minutes until brown. Yields 1 loaf.

This old steam cooking method requires more time, but it adds moisture to the bread. Because the bread contains no yeast, it doesn't need time to rise and is easy to make.

Recipe adapted from *The White House Cook Book* by Mrs. F.L. Gillette and Hugo Ziemann, 1887. *

☆ Bubble and Squeak

1 head of cabbage
4 tablespoons butter
½ pound corned beef
Salt and pepper to taste

Chop or shred the cabbage into small pieces. Melt butter in a pan and sauté the cabbage for 5 minutes. Chop corned beef into medium-size pieces and add to the pan. Sauté for 2 more minutes. Salt and pepper to taste. Serves 4.

Recipe adapted from *The White House Cook Book* by Mrs. F.L. Gillette and Hugo Ziemann, 1887. *

"Bubble and Squeak" was Cleveland's favorite dish. There are two versions of how this recipe was named—the first says while the cabbage is cooking, it bubbles and squeaks ... the second says it's related to the way a person's digestive system bubbles and squeaks after they've eaten it.

Benjamin Harrison

№ 23

Mrs. Harrison's Sausage Rolls

Original Recipe

Make a light biscuit dough (made with milk) and let it rise overnight. In the morning, roll it out thin and cut into shape with a biscuit cutter. In the center of each, place a roll of sausage the size of a good sized hickory nut and roll it up in the dough. After letting thins stand in the pan for a few minutes, bake and serve hot. These rolls are also good cold and when children have to take to school for luncheon in bad weather.

Recipe from *Statesmen's Dishes and How to Cook Them*, 1890.

Updated Recipe

¼ cup shortening or butter
2 cups sifted flour
2½ teaspoons baking powder
1 teaspoon salt
⅔ cup milk
12 small link sausages, cut into 1-inch pieces

Cut cold shortening or butter into the flour. Add baking powder, salt and milk. Mix with your hands to form a smooth dough. Roll the dough out thinly and cut into rectangles. Place a piece of sausage in the center of each and roll up in the dough. Bake 15–20 minutes at 450° F. Yields about 4 dozen. ★

While she lived in the White House, Caroline Harrison compiled a book of recipes, which were published as *Statesmen's Dishes and How to Cook Them*. She was also interested in the history of the mansion's furnishings and ordered an inventory.

She gathered all the miscellaneous pieces of china from previous administrations and started the White House China Collection. An artistic woman, Mrs. Harrison designed a new pattern for the state china using Indian corn and goldenrod. A teacher came from Indianapolis to teach china-painting classes, and a kiln was set up in the White House.

Mrs. Harrison's Fish Chowder ☆

1½ pounds shad or whitefish
3 to 4 potatoes
1 onion
¼ pound bacon
2 medium tomatoes
Salt and pepper to taste
1 pint milk
½ cup cracker crumbs

Cut the fish, potatoes, onion and bacon into small pieces. In a saucepan, fry the bacon and onions until light brown. Put a layer of potatoes in the pan, then a layer of fish, a sprinkling of onions and bacon, then a layer of tomatoes (chopped). Sprinkle with salt and pepper. Repeat layers until all is in.

Add enough water to cover; place over a moderate fire and let simmer 25 minutes. Boil (scald) the milk; thicken with cracker crumbs. Let it stand a moment and then add to the chowder. Now stir for the first time; let boil an instant. Season if not strong to taste, and serve hot.

Recipe from *Statesmen's Dishes and How to Cook Them*, 1890. ✱

President Harrison liked seafood and was especially fond of oysters. He even had his steward put them in his steak sauce.

Many Harrison family members lived in the White House including grandson Benny, who could not yet walk. Visitors reported feeling a warm arm around their ankles as the baby crawled about. At one conference, a roll of important papers disappeared, and the President began a frantic search. He discovered Benny behind the curtains, stirring a spittoon with the documents.

One of the most charming social events was a party for "Baby McKee's" fourth birthday. The President and Benny greeted guests in the East Room before leading them to the dining room. Around the table were 15 high chairs, and baskets of candy were set at each place.

Mrs. Harrison's Fig Pudding

1 cup black molasses
1 cup chopped suet
1 teaspoon cinnamon
½ teaspoon nutmeg
1 pint figs, finely chopped
1 teaspoon baking soda
1 tablespoon hot water
1 cup milk
2 eggs
3¼ cups flour

Mix together the molasses, suet, spices and figs. Dissolve the soda in hot water and mix with milk; add to the molasses mixture. Beat the eggs light and stir into the mixture; add the flour and beat thoroughly. Butter two small brown-bread molds or one large mold; turn the mixture into the mold and steam 5 hours. Serve with cream sauce.

Recipe from *Statesmen's Dishes and How to Cook Them*, 1890. ✳

When Benjamin Harrison moved into the White House, it was in such disrepair that plans were considered to tear it down and build a new mansion. Caroline herself drew up plans for new additions to the house. Congress didn't have the funds, and many citizens wanted to save the building, so renovations were begun. The First Lady supervised the modernizing of the kitchen. Bathrooms were added and rats exterminated.

According to one contemporary account, "The stories that Mrs. Harrison spends half her time in the kitchen actually taking part in the preparation of food are absurd, but she knows every detail of the household, and her servants adore her. No dusty corner in the big mansion escapes her eyes, and each item of the day's menu is discussed with the steward, who does the ordering and who supervises the domestic staff."

The Harrisons' social events had an elegant and festive atmosphere. The First Lady's decorations for large receptions included profuse amounts of plants and flowers.

On January 7, 1890, a dinner was given for Vice President Levi Morton and other Cabinet members. The East Room was festooned with miniature groves of palms, 2,000 azaleas, 900 hyacinths, 800 carnations, 400 lilies of the valley, 300 tulips, 300 roses, 200 bouvardias, 200 small fern plants, 100 sprays of asparagus fern and 40 poinsettias.

Mrs. Harrison's Clear Soup

4 pounds of juicy beef
1 knuckle of veal
2 small turnips
2 small carrots
1 soup bunch (herbs)
1 small pod of red pepper
2 small onions
Salt
6 quarts water

Boil 6 hours, then strain through a sieve. Let stand overnight and congeal—then skim off all the grease, put into a kettle to warm, and add sherry or Madeira wine to taste.

Recipe from *Statesmen's Dishes and How to Cook Them*, 1890. ★

The Harrisons put up the first decorated Christmas tree in the White House. The tree was set up in the oval room on the second floor. The family and staff all helped hang the ornaments, then the President dressed up as Santa Claus for his grandchildren.

President Harrison was a reserved person who often came across as dull. In contrast, his wife was lively and warm. Mrs. Harrison's secret to a flavorful turkey was to give the bird a walnut and a shot of sherry three times a day.

☆ Menu for the Harrison Family Christmas Dinner, 1889

Blue Point Oysters on the Half Shell
Consommé à la Royale
Chicken in Patty Shell
Stuffed Turkey
Duchess Potatoes   Braised Celery
Cranberry Jelly
Terrapin à la Maryland
Lettuce Salad with French Dressing
Mince Pie   American Plum Pudding
Tutti-Frutti Ice Cream
Ladyfingers   Macaroons   Carlsbad Wafers
Apples, Florida Oranges, Bananas, Grapes, Pears
Coffee

William McKinley

Mrs. McKinley's Corn Muffins

Original Recipe

1 egg, ½ cup cornmeal, one cup flour, teaspoon baking powder, two tablespoons granulated sugar, one cup sweet milk, two tablespoons butter, salt.

Recipe courtesy of The William McKinley Presidential Library & Museum. Published in *The Canton Favorite Cook Book,* compiled by the Ladies of the First Baptist Church, Canton, Ohio, 1896.

Updated Recipe

1 cup flour
½ cup cornmeal
2 tablespoons sugar
1 teaspoon baking powder
Pinch of salt
1 egg
1 cup whole milk
2 tablespoons butter, melted

Mix dry ingredients together. Beat eggs lightly and add to dry ingredients. Pour in milk and melted butter. Mix until everything is just moistened. Spoon mixture into muffin tins, filling two-thirds full. Bake at 425° F for 20 minutes or until done. Best served hot from the oven. Yields 6 muffins. ✲

William McKinley was devoted to his frail wife, Ida, who suffered from epilepsy. So he eliminated unnecessary entertaining, hosting large dinners instead of numerous small events. There were sometimes 100 dinner guests, and tables had to be set up in the corridor to accommodate everyone. The disadvantage of being seated in the hall was especially apparent in the winter. Whenever the front door was opened, gusts of icy wind blew in, so cushions were taken off the divans and used to warm the ladies' feet.

Both the President and First Lady enjoyed visiting the greenhouses on the White House grounds. Ida liked to pick red carnations to place in her husband's lapel. If McKinley had to decline a favor for someone, he would often take off his flower and pin it to the lapel of the other man.

Mrs. McKinley's White Layer Cake

Original Recipe

3 cups pulverized sugar, whites of six eggs, five cups flour, two heaping teaspoons baking powder, one cup sweet milk, one-half cup butter. Filling: One cup pulverized sugar, whites of two eggs beaten stiff. Add flavor to taste.

Recipe courtesy of The William McKinley Presidential Library & Museum. Published in *The Canton Favorite Cook Book,* compiled by the Ladies of the First Baptist Church, Canton, Ohio, 1896.

Updated Recipe

5 cups flour
2 rounded teaspoons baking powder
Pinch of salt
½ cup butter, softened
4 cups sugar
2 teaspoons vanilla
1 cup milk
8 egg whites

Grease and flour two 9" cake pans. Preheat oven to 350° F. Sift together flour, baking powder and salt. In a separate bowl, cream butter and 3 cups of sugar. Add 1 teaspoon of vanilla. Alternately beat milk and dry ingredients into the butter mixture. Whip 6 egg whites until stiff but not dry. Fold into batter. Pour into prepared cake pans. Bake for 30–35 minutes or until almost done. Cool on racks and remove from pans.

To make meringue filling, whip remaining egg whites until stiff. Continue beating, and slowly add remaining sugar and vanilla. Place the two cake layers on a cookie sheet. Spread filling evenly over the top of each cake. Bake at 200° F for 1 hour or until meringue is hard. Place one cake layer on a serving plate and put the other on top. Serves 8–10. ★

"Unlike any other nation, here the people rule, and their will is the supreme law. It is sometimes sneeringly said by those who do not like free government, that here we count heads. True, heads are counted, but brains also ..."

—*William McKinley*

The weather was sunny and bright on McKinley's inauguration day. A *New York Times* reporter wrote, "If good weather for so important an event may be accepted as a favorable augury, President McKinley has begun an administrative career that should be full of sunshine, good order, good humor and general satisfaction. Not a cloud cast its shadow over any part of the inaugural proceedings. The sun looked all day like a great disk of burnished gold."

After taking the oath of office, McKinley had a simple lunch—a corned beef sandwich, a salad and coffee. He ate with a few congressmen in a Senate committee room, and then headed to the White House to watch the inaugural parade.

During McKinley's administration, the White House was accessible to everyone, and the President thoroughly enjoyed entertaining and greeting people. He had a remarkable memory for faces, and his famous handshake made even his opponents go away with a favorable opinion.

The White House grounds were open and were used like a city park for strolling and picnicking. On summer evenings, the President could often be found enjoying a cigar on the South Portico.

President McKinley held public receptions three times a week. The people who attended were friendly, and McKinley felt that he got more out of the receptions than the attendees. "Everyone in the line has a smile and a cheery word," he said. "They bring no problems with them, only goodwill. I feel better after that contact."

A French chef was hired to cook for State Dinners (a second cook was employed to cook simpler food for the family). The number of courses varied from eight to 12. However, an impressive display was put on for the visit of President and Mrs. Sanford B. Dole from the Republic of Hawaii—71 courses were served!

Ironically, it was McKinley who cried out at a news conference, "What this country needs is a good 10-ounce can of condensed soup!" Shortly thereafter, the Campbell Soup Company introduced a 10½-ounce can of soup that sold for 10 cents.

Mrs. McKinley's Chicken Croquettes

Original Recipe

To the chopped chicken, add a little sage, then stir in the chicken gravy and some fine cracker crumbs; dip in a beaten egg, then in cracker crumbs and fry in hot lard.

> Recipe courtesy of The William McKinley Presidential Library & Museum. Published in *The Canton Favorite Cook Book,* compiled by the Ladies of the First Baptist Church, Canton, Ohio, 1896.

Updated Recipe

2 to 3 cups diced cooked chicken, cold
2 cups bread crumbs
½ teaspoon sage
Salt and pepper
1 teaspoon mustard
¼ cup butter, melted
1 egg, beaten
2 to 3 tablespoons oil
Parsley for garnish

Knead together the chicken, 1 cup of bread crumbs, sage, salt, pepper, mustard and butter until it resembles sausage meat. Form the mixture into cakes and dip them in beaten egg. Press them into the remaining bread crumbs. Fry in oil until they are light brown. Serve hot, garnished with sprigs of parsley. Serves 8. ✶

Tipsy Watermelon

15-pound watermelon
½ to ¾ cup light rum

Cut a 2-inch hole in the top of the watermelon. Dig out a deep plug of melon, and make several cuts into the inside flesh. Fill the hole with rum and allow the watermelon to sit for 8–10 hours. Turn it every few hours to ensure even distribution. ✶

The state of Georgia sent the President an unusual gift—a 78-pound prize watermelon. It was 2½ feet long and 6 feet in circumference. The melon was wrapped in an American flag and tied with a white ribbon. When Representative Livingston presented it to the President, he assured him, "No office seeker is enclosed within it."

Theodore Roosevelt

№ 26

Mrs. Roosevelt's Philadelphia Sand Tarts

Original Recipe

1 pound flour
1 pound sugar
½ pound butter
3 eggs (leaving out white of one)
Flavor vanilla
Roll thin

Brush surface with white egg. Sprinkle sugar and cinnamon.

These cookies were a family favorite, often served on Christmas morning.

Recipe courtesy of Sagamore Hill National Historic Site, Roosevelt's former home in Oyster Bay, New York.

Updated Recipe

1 cup butter
2 cups sugar
3 eggs
2 teaspoons vanilla
4 cups flour
Pinch of salt
½ teaspoon cinnamon plus 1 teaspoon sugar

Cream butter and sugar until light and fluffy. Add 2 eggs, beating after each one. Beat in vanilla and 1 additional egg yolk. Mix in flour and salt. Roll dough on a lightly floured board until thin. Cut out circles of dough, using a shot glass. Dip rim of glass in flour to keep dough from sticking. Beat remaining egg white slightly; brush over cookies. Mix cinnamon and sugar; sprinkle on top. Bake at 350° F for 7–10 minutes. Yields 50 cookies. ✶

Mrs. Roosevelt's Orange Marmalade

9 bitter and 3 sweet oranges, 4 lemons. Cut the fruit across the grain in very thin slices. Lay them for 24 hours in 4 quarts of water, boil for 2 hours then add 8 pounds of white sugar and boil for an hour or until it jellies. ✶

Theodore Roosevelt was a dynamic man who loved to hike and camp outdoors. He was a big game hunter and had a huge moose head installed over the fireplace in the State Dining Room. Other stuffed animal heads were hung around the room.

He was a passionate conservationist—never wanting a Christmas tree cut down and brought into the house. However, one year Archie smuggled a small tree into the White House, so on Christmas morning, the children weren't the only ones who were surprised.

Countess Cassini called the President a "gay showman—that terrific smile, a cannibal smile, that torturous grip which is his handshake. The Roosevelt stamp is already on the nation. He is ten men rolled into one. He never sits when he can stand, he never walks when he can run."

Edith Roosevelt held a sewing circle once a week with the wives of Cabinet members. The real purpose was to stay abreast of gossip. It was said her "sewing cabinet" made and unraveled many a political career.

One aide said the First Lady was "always the gentle, high-bred hostess: smiling often at what went on about her, yet never critical of the ignorant and tolerant always of the little insincerities of political life."

☆ Alice Roosevelt Longworth's Eggplant with Spaghetti or Rice

(President Roosevelt's Daughter)

Peel the eggplant; cut in thin slices; add a little salt to each slice; press under a heavy weight for ½ hour; fry in butter until tender; cook the spaghetti or rice; make tomato sauce; when ready to serve, put first in center of dish a layer of spaghetti or rice, a slice of eggplant, then another layer of spaghetti or rice, another slice of eggplant, and so on; pour the tomato sauce around the layers; serve. ∗

Alice Roosevelt, the oldest daughter, said her family preferred "coarse food and plenty of it." The President was a voracious eater and had a tremendous sweet tooth. He would put up to seven sugar cubes in his coffee cup, which his son described as "... more in the nature of a bathtub."

Alice was as beautiful as she was daring. She smoked on the White House roof, wore pants and was known to have a cocktail. Her wedding may have been the most lavish White House event ever. "Princess Alice" carried a bouquet of orchids that cascaded to the floor, and the train of her dress was 18 feet long. The wedding cake weighed 130 pounds.

The Roosevelt family was large and lively. They moved into the White House with their six children, governesses and the Irish cook from their home in New York.

The atmosphere in the mansion was informal, and the children were rarely disciplined. The boys called themselves "The White House Gang," and the President praised the inventiveness of his sons' pranks. They pitched tents on the lawn, played mock war games and splashed in the fountain.

Indoors, the long hallways were perfect for bicycle and stilt races. Kitchen trays were used to "sled" down the staircase, and once the children almost knocked down a visiting ambassador.

The East Room was used for roller-skating, but was declared off-limits when the boys attempted a water-pistol fight.

Once when little Archie was sick, the other children smuggled an Icelandic pony named "Algonquin" up the White House elevator to cheer him up.

Roosevelt loved to wrestle and have pillow fights with his boys. One of the only times he scolded them was when he discovered Quentin and his friend Charlie Taft (the son of the next President) shooting spitballs at the portrait of Andrew Jackson. Charlie was also known to

sneak under the table to tie guests' shoelaces together.

With all this activity, it's no surprise that the mansion seemed too small, so renovations were begun. The State Dining Room was enlarged, and the West Wing was built to hold the President's offices. At that point, the house still had no official name. Roosevelt referred to it as "the White House." He had stationery printed, and the name stuck.

Mrs. Roosevelt's Squash or Pumpkin Biscuit

Original Recipe

Two cups of milk, three quarters of a cup of sugar, warmed with butter the size of a walnut. Add it to two cups of boiled squash, one beaten egg, one half a yeast cake and one half a cup of warm water, with salt to taste, and flour enough to make a soft dough—Let it rise for six or seven hours and bake in muffin rings. A few raisins may be added if liked.

> Recipe courtesy of Sagamore Hill National Historic Site, Roosevelt's former home in Oyster Bay, New York.

Updated Recipe

2 eggs
¾ cup sugar
1 15-ounce can pumpkin or squash
3 tablespoons butter, melted
2 teaspoons baking powder
1 teaspoon baking soda
1 teaspoon cinnamon
½ teaspoon allspice
½ teaspoon nutmeg
Salt to taste

 1 12-ounce can evaporated milk
2½ cups flour, sifted
1 cup raisins (optional)

In a medium-size bowl, beat eggs lightly. Mix in sugar. Stir in pumpkin, butter, baking powder, baking soda, cinnamon, allspice, nutmeg and salt. Mix in half of the milk, then stir in half of the flour. Mix in remaining milk and flour. Add raisins if desired.

Generously grease and flour muffin tins. (Using paper liners is not recommended—muffins will stick.) Fill each muffin tin almost to the top. Bake at 400° F for 15 minutes. Reduce heat to 350° F and bake for about 30 minutes or until done. Serve hot. Yields 18 muffins. *

"Incidentally, I don't think any family has ever enjoyed the White House more than we have ... It is a wonderful privilege to have been here and to have been given the chance to do this work ..."

—Theodore Roosevelt

William H. Taft

№ 27

Runnymede Salad

2 long cucumbers
2 tablespoons butter
1 small portobello mushroom
1 cup small shrimp
½ cup boiled potato
½ cup artichoke bottoms
½ cup mayonnaise
3 tablespoons chutney

Wash cucumbers and cut a thick slice from each end. Cut each in three equal pieces and scoop out centers, leaving a cup. Melt butter in pan. Dice mushroom and sauté 3 minutes. Set aside 18 shrimp. Chop potato, artichokes and remaining shrimp into small pieces. Combine mayonnaise and chutney in a medium bowl; stir in chopped ingredients. Fill cucumber cups. Set on individual plates. Hang three reserved shrimp on the edge of each cucumber and put extra salad around bottom. Serves 6.

Adapted from *A New Book of Cookery* by Fannie Merritt Farmer, 1912. ★

When she became First Lady, Mrs. Taft remembered an earlier visit to Tokyo when all the cherry trees were in bloom. She conceived the idea of having the trees line the Tidal Basin in Washington.

American nurseries were only able to provide 80 trees, so the mayor of Tokyo donated 2,000 trees. Unfortunately, when they arrived at U.S. Customs, the trees were infested with fungus and bugs. The mayor then sent 2,000 replacements. On March 12, 1912, Mrs. Taft and the wife of the Japanese Ambassador attended the tree planting ceremony and dug the first shovel-full of dirt. The cherry trees remain one of Washington's loveliest landmarks.

When the Tafts' daughter, Helen, made her debut, a tea party for 1,200 people was given at the White House. There was also an elegant ball for 300, and for this event, a special band area was constructed on the roof of the East Wing. All the windowpanes and sashes were removed from the triple window of the East Room so the music could be heard and dancing could take place throughout the room.

William Howard Taft was by far the largest President, weighing around 325 pounds. "Big Bill" could not bend over to tie his shoes, so his valet did it for him. He got stuck several times in the White House bathtub and had to have his aides pull him out. His solution was to install a 7-foot-long tub that could hold four normal-size men.

When he served as Governor of the Philippines, Taft sent a cable to the Secretary of War, Elihu Root: "Took long horseback ride today; feeling fine." The response from Root was, "How is the horse?" Taft was so fat that Teddy Roosevelt once quipped that he should not go horseback riding, because it would be "dangerous for him and cruelty to the horse."

In spite of his weight, Taft was a good dancer. Helen also loved to dance, and they organized weekly dance lessons at the White House. They played records and danced the waltz and the two-step. Golf was another favorite recreation for the President, who practiced his strokes on the South Lawn, where his dog, "Laddy Boy," loved to retrieve the balls.

The Tafts enjoyed entertaining. They often had guests over for dinner and lunch—sometimes even breakfast. Not knowing exactly how many people would be there for a meal, the kitchen staff had instructions to keep extra provisions in stock at all times.

President Taft used entertaining to try and win support for his proposals. Occasionally two types of wine were served at dinner. If the President was seeking approval on an issue, the guest was served a vintage wine. Everyone else received an inferior brand.

"The nearer I get to the inauguration of my successor, the greater relief I feel."

—*William H. Taft*

Mrs. Taft's "A Dessert"

Original Recipe

1 cupful powdered sugar
6 egg yolks, beaten
2 teaspoons cocoa
1 teaspoonful prepared coffee
1 teaspoonful vanilla
6 egg whites, beaten very light

Mix all together. Bake in one thin pan in a moderate oven for ten minutes; beat cream very light; put it on the cake; roll up cake and cream; put chocolate icing over it; put whipped cream in stripes at the end.

Updated Recipe

6 eggs, separated
1 cup powdered sugar
1 teaspoon vanilla
2 tablespoons strong coffee
1 cup flour
1 teaspoon baking powder
2 teaspoons cocoa
¼ teaspoon salt
Chocolate Icing
½ cup butter
2 cups powdered sugar

 1 teaspoon vanilla
⅓ cup chocolate syrup
Pinch of salt
1 cup heavy cream, whipped

Beat egg yolks until thick. Pour sugar in slowly and beat until creamy. Stir in vanilla and coffee. Sift together the flour, baking powder, cocoa and salt. Add to egg mixture in thirds, beating after each addition. Beat egg whites to a stiff peak. Fold into batter. Grease a 9" x 13" pan and line with greased parchment paper. Pour batter into pan, spreading evenly to the edges. Bake at 350° F for 12–13 minutes or until done.

While cake is baking, cut an additional piece of parchment paper a little bigger than your pan. Lay it on the counter and smear it with a little powdered sugar. When cake is taken from the oven, you must work quickly. Loosen the sides of the cake with a spatula. Place second sheet of parchment over top of the cake, then invert the pan onto the counter. Remove pan and peel paper off bottom of cake. Trim off hard crusts.

While cake is cooling, make the icing. Cream together butter and sugar. Add vanilla and chocolate syrup. Beat until smooth. Spread over cake. Starting from one end, roll cake up to other end. If desired, dust top of cake with powdered sugar. Serve with whipped cream. ★

Deacon Porter's Hat

3 cups flour
1 teaspoon baking soda
1 teaspoon ginger
1 teaspoon cinnamon
½ teaspoon nutmeg
½ teaspoon cloves
1 cup butter
1 cup molasses
1 cup milk
½ cup chopped walnuts
½ cup raisins
Hard Sauce
¼ cup butter
2 tablespoons powdered sugar
1 teaspoon vanilla

Sift together the flour, baking soda and spices; set aside. Cream butter and mix with molasses and milk. Add the sifted ingredients and mix well. Add nuts and raisins; mix again. Pour into a greased 2-quart cylindrical mold. To steam the pudding, place the mold on a rack in a large pot. Pour boiling water into the pot to half the depth of the mold. Cover the pot and allow pudding to steam for 2 hours.

To make the hard sauce, cream butter and sugar, then add vanilla. Beat until light and smooth. Chill until serving time. Serve the pudding warm with hard sauce. Serves 10–12. ✱

 This dessert was a favorite of the Taft family. It was named after Deacon Porter, a trustee of Mount Holyoke College, where Mrs. Taft briefly attended classes. The pudding, which was served at the college on Thanksgiving, looks like the Deacon's stovepipe hat.

"I always said it would be a cold day when I got to be President." (There was a raging blizzard the night before the inauguration. Telephone, telegraph, trolley and railroad services were all disrupted, and the ceremony was held in the Senate chamber.)

—William H. Taft

Woodrow Wilson

Woodrow Wilson was an intellectual man who had served as president of Princeton University and later became Governor of New Jersey. In 1884, Wilson wrote in a letter to his wife, "A man who reads everything is like the man who eats everything: he can digest nothing, and the penalty for cramming one's mind with other men's thoughts is to have no thoughts of one's own."

Wilson could be aloof and self-righteous. William Allen White said his handshake was "like a ten-cent pickled mackerel in brown paper." But he had a lighter side and secretly thought he might have been successful in show business. The President sometimes entertained his family with a song or dance, and after State Dinners he often mimicked the people who had attended.

The President was also known to be inflexible and often refused to listen to contradictory views. England's ambassador, Walter Hines Page, was once so persistent that Wilson sprang up, stuck his fingers in his ears and ran out of the room.

Mrs. Wilson's Wine Jelly

3 lemons
4 packages of gelatin (unflavored)
2 pounds of granulated sugar
1 pint of good strong wine

Slice 1 lemon thin; set aside. Squeeze the juice from the other lemons and grate the peel of 1 lemon. Add 1 pint of cold water to the gelatin, then stir in 3 pints boiling water, sugar, wine, lemon juice, peel and lemon slices. Set in a cold place to congeal. Serves 10. ★

President Wilson's first wife, Ellen, was a good cook who trained herself because she wasn't satisfied with any of the cooks they hired. She was a poised and gracious hostess, but other than large State Dinners, the Wilsons usually only had close personal friends for dinner.

As First Lady, she took an interest in improving the slums of the nation's capital. Her involvement in social service activities led Maggie Rogers, a White House maid, to say, "I think we have an angel in the White House."

"Woodrow's Favorite" Charlotte Russe

Recipe from Mrs. Joseph Wilson (President Wilson's Mother)

2 tablespoons (envelopes) unflavored gelatin
½ cup water
4 egg yolks
½ cup sugar
2 cups milk
1 teaspoon vanilla
1 pint heavy cream
Maraschino cherries for garnish
Ladyfingers (optional)

Soak gelatin in water for about 5 minutes. Beat egg yolks slightly and add sugar. Scald milk; quickly stir in egg mixture (better to add a few drops of scalded milk to egg mixture, stirring constantly, then pour eggs into hot milk). Cook over medium (low) heat slowly, stirring constantly, until custard coats a spoon (about 5–10 minutes). Add gelatin and stir to blend well. Stir in vanilla and let cool.

Reserve 1 cup cream for garnish and fold remainder into custard mixture. Pour into a 2-quart mold.* Chill for 3–4 hours. Whip remaining cream.

 Serve dessert garnished with whipped cream and cherries. Serves 8.

*If desired, split ladyfingers or slices of sponge cake may be placed along the sides and bottom of a 3-quart mold and custard mixture poured on top.

Recipe from "Wilson Family Cook Book", a section in *The Economy Administration Cook Book,* 1913. "Woodrow's Favorite" is written on the page. *

Charlotte Russe was the dessert served at President Wilson's inaugural dinner. It was a simple affair for close family, 33 in all. Served in the State Dining Room, the meal also featured cream of celery soup, baked fillet of halibut with white sauce, roast capon, cauliflower, mashed potatoes, fruit salad and coffee.

Wilson was the first President to decline having an inaugural ball. Both he and Ellen were children of Presbyterian ministers, and they felt the frivolity of such an event would tarnish the sacredness of the occasion.

Mrs. Wilson said, "I would like to show that dinners and other social functions at the White House can be both beautiful and simple."

Mrs. Wilson's Pears in Cointreau with Frozen Cream

12 perfect firm Bartlett pears
Cold water, enough to cover pears
½ teaspoon lemon juice
4 cups light brown sugar
6 cups water
1 teacup Cointreau (4 to 6 ounces)
1 pint heavy cream

1. Peel the pears, leaving them whole with stems.
2. Put immediately in cold water to cover; add lemon juice to prevent them from turning brown.
3. Melt brown sugar and water in a 10-inch skillet and boil for 5 minutes, stirring.
4. Wipe pears dry. Add to sugar syrup and cook until transparent and tender, but not mushy.
5. Fill a teacup with Cointreau, and when the pears are done, lift each separately and dip in the Cointreau until well saturated.
6. Put them in a big glass dish, piling them in a pyramid if possible.
7. Continue to boil the syrup until it is moderately thick.
8. Add the Cointreau in which the pears were dipped. Stir and pour this mixture over the pears.
9. Place in refrigerator to chill.
10. One and a half hours before dinner is announced, empty the cream into a refrigerator tray. (Put cream in freezer for 1½ hours before serving.) When ready to serve the pears, this cream should be crystallized and not quite stiff.
11. Put the cream in a very cold silver bowl and pass with the pears.

Serves 12. ★

Two of the Wilsons' three daughters were married in the White House. The middle daughter, Jessie, married Francis B. Sayre, a law professor at Harvard. The groom almost missed his own wedding because he arrived at the White House without his invitation, and the guards were reluctant to let him proceed! The couple had a magnificent wedding in the East Room in November 1913. The wedding cake was 3 feet in diameter and weighed 130 pounds.

The youngest daughter, Eleanor, married William Gibbs McAdoo, the Secretary of the Treasury, in May of 1914. The wedding was much smaller, due to the ill health of their mother. Wilson was devastated when Ellen died that same year.

War Bread

1 cup rye meal
1 cup graham flour
½ cup white flour (unsifted)
1 teaspoon cream of tartar
1 teaspoon baking soda
1 teaspoon salt
¼ cup molasses
1⅛ cups sour milk (buttermilk)
1 egg, well beaten
2 tablespoons melted shortening
½ cup raisins

Mix dry ingredients. Combine molasses, sour milk, egg and shortening; stir into flour mixture. Stir in raisins. Pour into a greased 10" x 4" x 3" bread pan and bake at 375° F for 50 minutes or until done. Yields 1 loaf.

Recipe courtesy of The Woodrow Wilson House, Washington, D.C. ★

After his wife's death, Wilson met a charming young widow named Edith Galt. She rejected his initial proposal of marriage, but he courted her "with Secret Service men behind every tree."

As World War I loomed closer, Woodrow said he could not ask her to share the burden of his office. Edith flung her arms around him and replied, "Well, if you won't ask me, I will

 volunteer, and be ready to be mustered in as soon as possible."

They were married in a small ceremony at Edith's house, followed by a honeymoon in Hot Springs, Virginia.

After America declared war on Germany in 1917, the American people were encouraged to economize by observing days without meat, heat or gasoline. The White House joined these efforts and eliminated many nonessential items from their menus.

President Wilson kept sheep on the White House grounds to act as lawn mowers. The sheep's wool was used to make army blankets. One ram nicknamed "Ike" liked to chew tobacco.

Warren G. Harding

№ 29

Senate Bean Soup

1 pound navy (pea) beans
3 quarts water
1 meaty ham bone
3 small onions, finely chopped
3 celery stalks, finely chopped
1 cup mashed potatoes
2 cloves garlic, minced
¼ cup chopped parsley

Place beans in a large pot and add water to cover them. Soak beans overnight. Drain. Put 3 quarts water and ham bone into pot along with the beans. Bring to a boil, skim, then cover pot and simmer for about 1 hour, stirring occasionally. Add remaining ingredients and simmer 1 more hour. Remove ham bone and cut meat into bite-size pieces. Return meat to soup and serve. *

This soup has been served on Capitol Hill since 1904, when House Speaker "Uncle Joe" Cannon bellowed, "From now on, hot or cold, rain, snow or shine, I want it on the menu every day!"

Warren Harding was an easygoing man, although he wasn't particularly bright or imaginative. He spoke somewhat awkwardly and sometimes mixed up words or verb tenses.

Florence Harding was a strong-willed woman who had helped run the circulation department of Harding's newspaper, *The Daily Star.* She watched the budget carefully and occasionally spanked the newsboys.

When her husband was nominated for President, she worked tirelessly on his campaign. She took credit for his election and once said to him, "Well, Warren, I have got you the Presidency: what are you going to do with it?"

"My God, this is a hell of a job! I have no trouble with my enemies ... but my damn friends, they're the ones that keep me walking the floor nights."

—*Warren Harding*

Eggplant Salad

1 dozen eggplants, each about 4 to 5 inches
Salt and pepper
Sprinkling of paprika
¼ cup butter
3 tablespoons mayonnaise
1 tablespoon vinegar
Juice of 1 lemon
½ teaspoon Worcestershire sauce
1 teaspoon bottled salsa
Lettuce leaves
2 hard-boiled eggs

Peel the eggplants and cut them into slices about ½ inch thick. Season with salt, pepper and paprika. Place them on a baking sheet. Put a dab of butter on each, and bake at 400° F for 8 minutes. Turn slices over and put a dab of butter on the other side. Bake for an additional 8 minutes or until tender.

In a separate bowl, mix the mayonnaise, vinegar, lemon juice, Worcestershire sauce and salsa. Add salt and pepper to taste. Marinate the eggplant in this sauce for several hours. Arrange lettuce on a serving plate and put eggplant in the middle. Finely chop the eggs and sprinkle over the top. Serves 10. ★

☆ Bird's Nest Salad

Rub a little green coloring paste into cream cheese, giving it a delicate color like bird's eggs. Roll it into balls the size of bird's eggs, using the back or smooth side of butter-pats. Arrange on a flat dish some small well-crimped lettuce leaves; group them to look like nests, moisten them with French dressing, and place five of the cheese balls in each nest of leaves. The cheese may be varied by flecking them with black, white or red pepper.

Recipe from *The Century Cook Book* by Mary Ronald, 1895. ★

President and Mrs. Harding loved to entertain and held many formal and informal parties. When it was time for the guests to leave a party, the Marine Band would play "The End of a Perfect Day."

The Hardings kept toothpicks on the table and tried to present themselves as "just folks," but soon after the inauguration, the First Lady had the White House silverware sent off to be triple gold-plated. The entertainment bills were so high that the Hardings economized by turning off every other lightbulb.

Bourbon Balls

1 cup pecans, finely chopped
1 cup vanilla wafers, crushed
1½ cups confectioners' sugar
2¼ cups cocoa
⅛ teaspoon ground cloves
⅓ cup bourbon
1½ tablespoons corn syrup

Mix pecans, vanilla wafers, 1 cup confectioners' sugar, cocoa and cloves in a medium-size bowl. Mix bourbon and corn syrup together. Add to dry ingredients. Mix well. Form 1-inch balls from the dough. Roll in remaining confectioners' sugar. Store in airtight container for a few days before serving. Yields 2 dozen cookies. *

"I love these beautiful big rooms with their high ceilings, their wide spaces, their polished mahogany furniture, carved deep with memories of Lincoln and the Madisons."

—*Florence Harding*

Breakfast Dish

Cut smoothly from a wheaten loaf
Ten slices, good and true,
And brown them nicely, o'er the coals,
As you for toast would do.

Prepare a pint of thickened milk,
Some cod-fish shredded small;
And have on hand six hard-boiled eggs,
Just right to slice withal.

Moisten two pieces of the bread,
And lay them in a dish,
Upon them slice a hard-boiled egg,
Then scatter o'er with fish.

And for a seasoning you will need
Of pepper just one shake,
Then spread above the milky juice,
And this one layer make.

And thus, five times, bread, fish and egg,
Or bread and egg and fish,
Then place one egg upon the top,
To crown this breakfast dish.

Elizabeth W. Stanton
The Woman Suffrage Cook Book,
1886

Harding's administration was filled with dishonesty and is considered one of the most corrupt. Publicly, the President obeyed the 18th Amendment, which outlawed alcohol. However, when he entertained friends in the private apartments of the White House, they often played cards and drank Scotch.

The First Lady poured drinks, and the men called her "The Duchess." Harding loved to snack on green onions, and the men dined on knockwurst and sauerkraut. In one game, Harding lost a priceless set of White House china that had belonged to Benjamin Harrison.

Despite his drinking, gambling, smoking and adultery, President Harding had a strong belief in God. This did not stop his immoral behavior, but when he went to church, he would not take Communion because he felt unworthy.

The President loved to go horseback riding on Sunday mornings. Florence always insisted he return in time for church. A Secret Service man accompanied him on his rides and was instructed to make sure he didn't take the long road home.

Harding did not like being President and once confessed to his mistress, Nan Britton, "I'm in jail, and I can't get out. I've got to stay."

Calvin Coolidge

№ 30

Mrs. Coolidge's Lemon Pie

2 eggs, separated
1 cup sugar
2 tablespoons flour
Juice of 1 lemon
1 tablespoon butter, melted
Pinch of salt
Pastry for 9-inch pie

Beat egg yolks lightly. Stir in sugar and flour. Add lemon juice, butter and salt. Fold in stiffly beaten egg whites. Line a 9-inch pie pan with pastry and bake at 450° F for 10 minutes. Pour in the filling and bake at 325° F for 30 minutes or until filling is set. Serves 8. ★

Mrs. Coolidge loved living in the White House and crocheted a bedspread for the Lincoln bed. She completed one square every month they were in the mansion.

Coolidge reportedly slept more than any other President, taking two- to four-hour naps in the afternoons. For recreation, he liked to ride a mechanical bull, which was in the bedroom.

Mrs. Coolidge's Icebox Cookies

1 cup butter or Crisco (if Crisco, use a little less and salt it)
2 cups brown sugar
3½ cups flour
1 teaspoon (baking) soda
½ teaspoon salt
1 cup nut meats
2 eggs, well beaten

Cream butter and sugar. Sift flour, soda and salt three times. Add nuts, eggs and flour mixture to butter mixture. Mix all thoroughly and pack into mold (long narrow bread pan) and let stand overnight (in refrigerator). Next day, unmold, slice very thin, and bake in moderate oven (375° F for 10–12 minutes). Do not grease mold or baking pan. ★

One of the thriftiest Presidents, Coolidge looked over menus and accounts in an effort to eliminate extravagances. He reduced the amount of meat served at State Dinners. Breakfast meetings were preferred because they were cheaper than lunch or dinner.

Coolidge hosted a series of "alphabetical breakfasts." Congressmen were invited alphabetically according to their last name. About 12 members attended each breakfast, and the menu was always the same: sausage, bacon, eggs, buckwheat pancakes, corn muffins, grapefruit, toast and coffee.

At one political breakfast, guests were surprised to see the President pour some of his coffee and cream into a saucer. To be polite, a few guests did the same. They waited for Coolidge to take a sip, but he put his saucer on the floor for the cat.

He was also thrifty with his time, even to the point of having his haircut while eating breakfast.

The President's one extravagance was clothing for his wife. He loved to buy her brightly colored outfits and never wanted to see her in the same dress for state functions. Mrs. Coolidge often had to get his approval before purchasing clothes. He was a jealous husband and got angry if she arrived home later than expected.

☆ Mrs. Coolidge's Coffee Soufflé

1 tablespoon butter
1 tablespoon flour
¾ cup strong coffee
⅓ cup milk
3 eggs, separated
¼ teaspoon salt
⅓ cup sugar
½ teaspoon vanilla
1 cup heavy cream, whipped

Melt butter in top of double boiler over boiling water. Add flour and mix until smooth. Slowly add coffee, stirring until smooth. Mix in milk. Beat egg yolks slightly and stir in salt and sugar. Add to coffee mixture. Stirring constantly, cook until it thickens and coats the spoon. Remove from the heat and add vanilla. Cool about 10 minutes.

Butter a 9-inch soufflé dish. Dust with powdered sugar. Beat egg whites until stiff. Fold into coffee mixture. Pour into soufflé dish. Bake at 350° F for about 30–35 minutes. Serve immediately with whipped cream. Serves 4–6.

Adapted from Mrs. Coolidge's recipe. ★

Calvin Coolidge was quiet and subdued, especially at large gatherings. It was once said that whenever he opened his mouth, a moth flew out. The President didn't like unnecessary conversation, but he was a master of short quips and known for his dry sense of humor.

He said, "If you don't say anything, you can't be called on to repeat it."

At one dinner party, a guest bet that she could get "Silent Cal" to say at least three words to her. Coolidge's reply was, "You lose." On another occasion, a senator pointed to the White House and said, "Wonder who lives there." Coolidge remarked, "No one. They just come and go."

In contrast, Grace Coolidge was lively and very popular. She had worked at a school for the deaf before her marriage, so she said she was used to quiet people.

Mrs. Coolidge initially struggled to learn how to cook—her baked items were a bit heavy, and her husband teased her by dropping a biscuit and stomping his foot at the moment it hit the floor. But she eventually became accomplished in the kitchen.

"I, and yet, not I—this was the wife of the President of the United States, and she took precedence over me."

—*Grace Coolidge*

Minted Chicken

2 limes
1 tablespoon fresh mint
1 tablespoon fresh cilantro
1 tablespoon butter
1 tablespoon oil
6 chicken breasts
1 cup chicken broth
¼ teaspoon ground cloves
Salt and pepper to taste
1 tablespoon preserved ginger, chopped
1 tablespoon cornstarch
3 tablespoons water

Squeeze juice from limes. Chop mint and cilantro and put into lime juice; set aside. Put butter and oil in pan. Brown chicken over medium heat. Slowly add chicken broth. Stir in cloves, salt, pepper and ginger. Cover and simmer 20 minutes or until done. Dissolve cornstarch in water and add to pan. Mix well with pan juices. Cook 5 minutes or until sauce thickens. Serves 6. ★

 Coolidge was so fond of chicken that he had a chicken coop built behind the White House. These chickens had a wonderfully mysterious flavor, and it was later discovered that the chicken yard was built on top of Teddy Roosevelt's mint patch.

Calvin and Grace were fond of a variety of foods, including Chinese. When the President retired to "The Beeches" in Northampton, Massachusetts, Mrs. Coolidge wrote out a list of instructions to her staff. One part read, "Do not hesitate to try new recipes. We like surprises. Good cooking requires time, study, material and experimentation."

Coolidge strictly observed the formal customs of the presidency, insisting his family wear full evening attire for dinner, even if there were no guests.

One dinner for the President of Cuba nearly turned into a disaster. One guest's bow tie fell off during dinner ... another cracked a front tooth ... and a third man broke through the seat of his cane chair. When he stood up, the chair was stuck on his backside. Meanwhile, there was a fire in the chimney. The staff scurried about the White House roof to extinguish the flames.

Herbert Hoover

№ 31

Herbert Hoover was from a humble background. He had worked his way through college to become a mining engineer. A smart businessman, he was a millionaire by the age of 40. The Hoovers entertained lavishly and frequently, and if expenses went over budget, Hoover paid the difference himself.

Guests were so frequent that Hoover and his wife, Lou, rarely ate a meal by themselves. Sometimes there was a luncheon, two teas and a dinner in one day. Many invitations were made at the last minute, so the staff never knew how many places to set.

Hoover was a Quaker, so all dancing was banned from the White House. The only exception was a party given for one of the couple's sons.

In his first open house, on New Year's Day, the President shook hands with 3,000 people before abruptly leaving the room. His hand was bruised and had been cut by people's rings. The next year, the Hoovers announced they would be out of town for New Year's Day. Thus ended the custom of holding an open house.

Mrs. Hoover's Venison

Moose, elk, reindeer, bear meat, or any tough or dry meat. (As frequently cooked by mountain folk.)

Fashion into small cutlets; dip in olive oil; fry in deep fat exactly like doughnuts until done as you like (perhaps 5 minutes, but you had better experiment with a small bit first).

Sprinkle with salt and pepper. Serve instantly. (The cutlet may first be rolled in bread crumbs, cornmeal or batter. But this makes them much greasier.)

Recipe courtesy of the Herbert Hoover Presidential Library. ★

Mrs. Hoover's Rolled Toast

Cut very thin slices of bread that will roll up without crumbling. Spread with soft butter. Starting at one corner, roll bread as tightly as possible without breaking the bread. Fasten by piercing with a wooden toothpick. Toast slowly. Remove toothpick and serve. (May first be spread with cheese, cinnamon and sugar, maple sugar or any conserve.)

Recipe courtesy of the Herbert Hoover Presidential Library. ★

Lou Henry Hoover was an accomplished linguist who could speak four languages fluently, and could read and write two more. She was an active Girl Scout leader—helping raise almost $2 million and increasing the membership from 100,000 to almost a million.

She encouraged women to be active volunteers or pursue a career. Mrs. Hoover urged her husband to open up more civil service jobs for women, and she also encouraged boys in 4-H clubs to help with housework.

Although the First Lady spoke about the importance of homemaking, she herself rarely cooked. "Mrs. Hoover's Venison" and "Mrs. Hoover's Rolled Toast" are her only known recipes.

When her husband lost his bid for reelection, Mrs. Hoover politely took the incoming First Lady, Eleanor Roosevelt, on a tour of the White House. They stopped at the door to the kitchen, where Mrs. Hoover said that the housekeeper would have to show Mrs. Roosevelt the kitchens—she had never entered them.

 Orange Jelly

Recipe from Mary Wasley Minthorn (President Hoover's Grandmother)

3 oranges
1 lemon
11 cups water
7 cups sugar

Cut oranges and lemon into small pieces, add water and let stand 24 hours. Boil 5 to 10 minutes, let stand 24 hours. Add sugar. Boil until thick. (Seal in jars according to manufacturer's directions.)
Recipe courtesy of the Herbert Hoover Presidential Library. *

When the Hoovers celebrated their first Christmas in the White House, their grandchildren were living with them while their father, Herbert Hoover Jr., was recovering from tuberculosis.

A Christmas tree was set up, and real cookies were used for decorations. There was a feast for 50 guests. Each lady received a bell as a souvenir, while the gentlemen received brass candlesticks.

Mary's Caramel Tomatoes

Recipe from Mary Ratley (The Hoover Family Cook)

Cut off the tops of six tomatoes—leave the stem—and make a cavity in the top. Fill each hole with a good-sized piece of butter—not a stingy piece—and put a tablespoonful of sugar on each tomato. Sprinkle with salt, and put in the oven to cook until the sugar is brown and the tomato done but not flat. Stick a sprig of parsley in the top of each tomato and serve on rounds of toast with the sauce that collects at the bottom of the pan.

Recipe courtesy of the Herbert Hoover Presidential Library. ★

Hoover did not have a big appetite. "I'm an engineer and I'm not using my body," he said. "An engineer does not stoke the engine unless there is a considerable amount of power to be exerted. So, I eat as little as I can to get along." A very fast eater, he once finished a full seven-course dinner in eight minutes.

Mrs. Hoover loved orange juice and drank three glasses a day. She kept a container of it on her nightstand.

The Hoovers had very strict rules for the staff, and the First Lady insisted that all the waiters had to be the same height. She made one exception for a young man named Alonzo Fields. At 6-foot-4, he towered over the other waiters, but he was so good at his job that she kept him on.

At formal dinners, the waiters stood stiffly at attention and waited for the First Lady to signal instructions. For example, if she touched her hair, it was time to announce dinner.

The President wanted the staff to be as invisible as possible. If he was coming down the hall, the staff was alerted to jump into the nearest closet until he had passed. Likewise, the gardeners were instructed to hide behind a bush or tree.

Presidential Corned-Beef Hash ☆

4 medium-sized potatoes
½ cup hot milk
2 rounded tablespoons butter
2 tablespoons chopped celery
2 tablespoons chopped green pepper
2 tablespoons chopped white onion
2 cups minced corned beef (fat and gristle removed)
Salt and pepper to taste

Boil potatoes until soft. Mash the potatoes and gradually add the hot milk and butter. Stir in celery, green pepper, onion and corned beef. Mix all ingredients thoroughly. Add salt and pepper to taste. Bake in a greased pan at 350° F for 30 minutes or until rich golden brown. Add tomato sauce, described below. Serves 6. ★

Tomato Sauce

2 tablespoons butter
1 onion, finely chopped
1 clove garlic, minced
3 tomatoes, chopped
Salt and pepper to taste
1 teaspoon sugar
2 teaspoons tomato paste
1 teaspoon flour
1½ cups water

Heat butter in a pan. Add onion, garlic, tomatoes, salt, pepper and sugar. Cook briskly for 10 minutes, stirring occasionally. Add tomato paste, flour and water. Stir until it comes to a boil. Simmer ½ hour. Pour over the corned-beef hash on a hot platter.

Recipe from Katherine Buckley, White House Cook. Courtesy of the Herbert Hoover Presidential Library. ★

Corned-beef hash was a favorite dish of five Presidents. Katherine Buckley, the White House cook, said this dish "... will put the crossest husband in a good humor!"

Although Hoover enjoyed gourmet meals, he maintained his love of simple foods, such as corn bread, baked beans and sweet potatoes with marshmallows. He liked ham, too, but his doctor advised him to go on a low-salt diet. When his wife was away, he conspired with the chef to serve ham.

He once said, "When I ate the worst, my thoughts went back to Iowa, and when I ate the best, I was still sure that Aunt Millie was a better cook ... if all the cooks of Iowa are up to Aunt Millie's standard, then the gourmets of the world should leave Paris for Iowa, at least for Cedar County."

Franklin D. Roosevelt

№ 32

Mrs. Roosevelt's Scrambled Eggs

1 tablespoon butter
6 eggs
3 tablespoons cream
½ teaspoon salt

Melt butter in pan, stir in eggs and cream beaten lightly together. (Add salt. Cook over medium heat. When eggs are set, transfer to serving dish. Serves 3–5.) ★

Mrs. Roosevelt's Toasted Cheese Sandwich

White sauce
1 pound strong store cheese, grated
Paprika
Toast

Make a thin white sauce, add cheese gradually and cook until thoroughly melted to a smooth consistency. Sprinkle with paprika and serve on toast. ★

"Martha Washington's Crab Soup"

2 tablespoons butter
1 tablespoon flour
2 hard-boiled eggs, mashed
Grated peel of 1 lemon
1 quart milk or light cream or half-and-half
1½ pounds crabmeat, cut in large pieces
1 teaspoon Worcestershire sauce
1 teaspoon onion juice
½ teaspoon salt
¼ teaspoon pepper
½ cup sherry

Blend butter and flour in double boiler; add the mashed eggs and lemon peel. Add milk and stir until thick. Add crabmeat and simmer 5 minutes. Add seasonings. Just before serving, stir in sherry and heat through. Serves 8. ★

Mrs. Washington may have served this soup to her husband, George. The soup was a favorite of the Roosevelts.

Franklin Delano and Eleanor Roosevelt were part of a large extended family, and the White House was often the setting for their gatherings. The children and grandchildren referred to the President and Mrs. Roosevelt as "Pa" and "Ma."

Sunday dinner was an informal meal. A silver chafing dish was placed next to Mrs. Roosevelt's seat at the table, and she made scrambled eggs for everyone. She once confessed that this was the only dish she knew how to make. Sunday dinners also included cold cuts, shoestring potatoes, fruit, cheese and crackers. The President appointed himself in charge of cocktails, and he often whipped up a batch of martinis while Eleanor scrambled the eggs.

While they lived in the White House, the Roosevelts received many gifts of fowl and game. The President liked to carve the meat himself to make sure none of it went to waste. FDR discovered that moose meat was delicious when served with grape jelly.

☆ Kedgeree

1 cup boiled flaked whitefish
1 cup cooked rice
¼ cup cream (or ¼ cup fish stock)
2 tablespoons butter
½ teaspoon salt
Dash of pepper
2 to 3 hard-boiled eggs, chopped
Parsley for garnish

Mix the fish with the rice. Moisten with cream or fish stock, and sauté lightly in melted butter. The fish must stay light and fluffy. Add salt, pepper and chopped eggs. Heat in top of double boiler. Serve hot, garnished with parsley. ★

Made from leftover fish, kedgeree was an ideal recipe for times of rationing. It was one of Eleanor's favorites.

Families had to be thrifty during this era—both the Great Depression and World War II occurred during FDR's term, which, at 12½ years, was the longest of any President.

Curried Chicken

Recipe from Mrs. James Roosevelt (President Roosevelt's Mother)

2 tablespoons butter
2 onions, chopped
2 teaspoons flour
2 teaspoons curry powder
2 cups chicken broth
½ apple, grated
1 large carrot, grated
4 chicken breasts, cut up

Melt butter in pan and sauté onions until golden. Add flour and curry and blend until smooth. Cook 3 minutes. Slowly add chicken broth, stirring to make a smooth sauce. Add remaining ingredients and cook, uncovered, over medium heat for 45 minutes to 1 hour or until chicken is done. *

Roosevelt was not a picky eater, but several times he complained to the housekeeper, Henrietta Nesbitt, about being served the same food over and over. He was once given liver and beans for three days, and another time he had chicken five days in a row.

He said, "I'm getting to the point where my stomach positively rebels, and this does not help my relations with foreign powers. I bit two of them today."

Ernest Hemingway said the White House food was, "The worst I've ever eaten. We had rainwater soup, followed by rubber squash, a nice wilted salad and a cake some admirer had sent in. An enthusiastic but unskilled admirer."

In spite of the complaints about the food, Mrs. Roosevelt refused to fire Mrs. Nesbitt. The lack of variety of dishes was due in part to the food rationing in effect during the war.

"Prime meats are supposed to be the backbone of American cuisine," commented Mrs. Nesbitt, "but we proved we could work our way around them when war and rationing came along, and the leaders of the world were gathered in the White House working night and day toward peace ... Boiled tongue became a favorite standby, since it was easier to get than most meats, and so was corned beef, which proved to be a lifesaver. We cooked it with cabbage the first day, and the beef did double duty next day as hash."

"The Presidency is not merely an administrative office. That's the least of it. It is more than an engineering job, efficient or inefficient. It is preeminently a place of moral leadership."
—*Franklin D. Roosevelt*

Chicken Soup à L'Amande

1 pint rich milk
1 teaspoon onion juice (or garlic juice)
¼ teaspoon pepper
¾ teaspoon salt
Bay leaf
3 cups chicken stock
½ cup blanched and ground almonds
1 tablespoon butter
1 tablespoon flour
½ pint (heavy) cream, (whipped)

Add milk and seasoning to the chicken stock, and some of the almonds. Blend butter and flour and add to this. Be sure there are no lumps. Bring to boiling point but no further. Serve with whipped cream on top of each serving sprinkled with ground almonds. One of our "party soups" for luncheon. Serves 10.

Recipe from *The Presidential Cookbook* by Henrietta Nesbitt, © 1951 by Henrietta Nesbitt. Used by permission of Doubleday, a division of Random House, Inc. *

Eleanor Roosevelt spent a great deal of time selecting menus, but she ate little herself. "She was too much interested in talk to care what she ate—she'd eat anything put before her," said Henrietta Nesbitt. If Mrs. Roosevelt had an appointment to keep, she ordered a light lunch, such as fruit and a bowl of "Chicken Soup à L'Amande."

Mrs. Roosevelt had tremendous energy and traveled an average of 40,000 miles a year. She was very involved in social welfare and reported her keen observations back to the President.

"If you lived your life trying to make sure that nobody ever criticized you, you would probably never get out of bed—and you'd be criticized for that!"
—*Eleanor Roosevelt*

In the beginning of his administration, the Roosevelts entertained often, and Eleanor organized a group to dance the Virginia reel in the East Room. Once the war began, many events were suspended, but receptions for servicemen were held about three times a week. The refreshments included pretzels, chips, cookies, punch and beer.

When he was Governor of New York, Roosevelt often pressed his guests to have a second or third drink. A favorite was his "Haitian Libation," made with orange juice, rum and grenadine.

At the sight of a guest's empty glass, he inquired, "How about another little sippy?" This likely explains the wilting houseplants—soil analysis revealed a high alcohol content (guests had emptied their drinks into the plants).

The King and Queen of England visited the White House in 1939. Before they arrived, the mansion went into a frenzy of activity. Each of the guest rooms was completely redecorated. Samples of London drinking water were analyzed so the White House water could be adjusted accordingly.

Buckingham Palace had sent pages of instructions for the comfort of King George VI and his entourage. Requirements included specific colored pens, a certain type of glass for the King's bathroom, and directions for folding the blanket at the foot of Queen Elizabeth's bed.

The royal couple was taken to Springwood, the Roosevelt mansion in Hyde Park, New York, for a picnic. The Roosevelts treated them to a truly American dish—hot dogs! Smoked turkey, ham, baked beans and strawberry shortcake were among the other foods served.

FDR also invited them to Val-Kill Cottage for swimming and tea. After the President got out of the pool, he wanted to cross the lawn, but he didn't want to be carried by a Secret Service man (his legs had been paralyzed by polio since the age of 39). So Roosevelt moved across the lawn in a crab-like way, by sitting backward on the ground and using his arms to swing his body ahead.

Unfortunately, a waiter had set a tray on the ground, and Roosevelt soon found himself sitting amid pastries and broken china. He laughed at himself, but then turned to the King and said, "… it's as funny as a crutch."

"A good leader can't get too far ahead of his followers."

—*Franklin D. Roosevelt*

Boiled Salmon with Egg Sauce ☆

Select the heavy part of a good-sized salmon, about 4 pounds. Wrap in muslin and boil in deep kettle in 3 quarts water containing ½ cup vinegar and ¼ cup salt. A 4-pound piece of fish will take about 30 minutes. Serve with Egg Sauce.

Make a white sauce of 2 cups cream or milk, 2 tablespoons butter, 2 tablespoons flour, ½ teaspoon salt, and dash black pepper. Add 3 hard-boiled eggs cut fairly small. Serves 8.

Recipe from *The Presidential Cookbook* by Henrietta Nesbitt, © 1951 by Henrietta Nesbitt. Used by permission of Doubleday, a division of Random House, Inc. ∗

Roosevelt considered salmon to be the king of fish, according to Henrietta Nesbitt. His other favorite foods were fish chowder, kedgeree, Italian rice, fruitcake, pumpkin pie, oranges, strawberries Romanoff and pecan pie.

The President ate breakfast in bed, and Mrs. Nesbitt made sure that a biscuit was always put on the tray for his dog, "Fala."

Roosevelt also liked to eat sauerkraut with pigs' knuckles. This was once served to Winston Churchill, who later said, "The pickled cabbage would have been tolerable had it not been for those damned pigs' knuckles leering at me."

Churchill felt comfortable visiting the White House ... so comfortable, in fact, that he often wandered the hallways in the nude. The staff quickly adjusted and kept their eyes on the ground when they passed.

During one visit, the President knocked on Churchill's door and was told to enter. When he went in, FDR was embarrassed at Churchill's nudity and started to back out of the room. Churchill threw out his arms and proclaimed, "Come in, Mr. President! The Prime Minister of England has nothing to conceal from the President of the United States!"

The Gridiron Club, a newspapermen's organization, organized an annual dinner for the President. This event was for men only and featured skits that poked fun at political figures. Eleanor started a "Gridiron Widows' Party" for women only on the same night.

She and her daughter, Anna, performed an original skit, featuring Mrs. Roosevelt as an old woman selling apples. She wore a sunbonnet and shawl and complained about her troubles. Anna appeared in a devil costume and transformed the old woman into a First Lady for a day.

The "First Lady" compared the difficulties of each situation, and decided she'd rather revert back to being an apple seller. The skit was a huge success and drew much laughter from the ladies.

Harry Truman

№ 33

Mrs. Truman's Brownies

1½ cups flour
½ teaspoon salt
1 cup softened butter
2 cups sugar
4 eggs
2 teaspoons vanilla
4 squares unsweetened chocolate
1 cup walnut or pecan pieces

Sift together flour and salt. Cream the butter and gradually beat in the sugar. Mix until light and fluffy. Add eggs and vanilla and beat until smooth. Melt chocolate in top of double boiler, then add to butter mixture. Stir in flour mixture, then add the nuts. Bake in a well-greased 8" square pan at 350° F for about 40 minutes. Cool before cutting. *

Mrs. Truman was a very good cook, but she was also very secretive about her recipes. This is probably her recipe for brownies.

The family preferred simple food that was well prepared. Truman called himself a "meat-and-potatoes man," but the only things he truly disliked were cucumbers and onions. He could always tell if a dish had even a small amount of onion and would push it aside.

Mrs. Truman disliked being in the spotlight, and her reserved manner made her seem cold. She was terrified of becoming First Lady and said, "I don't know what I'm going to do. I'm not used to this awful public life."

She eventually settled into her role but never really liked it. However, she was warm and witty around her family. Chief Usher J.B. West described her sense of humor as "... dry, laconic, incisive and very funny." She could make the President and their daughter howl with laughter.

"I was very apprehensive. The country was used to Eleanor Roosevelt. I couldn't possibly be anything like her—I wasn't going down in any coal mines."

—*Bess Truman*

Mrs. Truman's Blarney Stones ☆

6 egg whites
½ teaspoon cream of tartar
1½ cups sugar
6 egg yolks, beaten well
1 cup cake flour, sifted before measuring
½ teaspoon vanilla flavoring
½ teaspoon lemon flavoring
¼ pound butter (very soft)
2 cups confectioners' sugar, sifted
1 egg, beaten*

Beat egg whites and cream of tartar until stiff. Fold in sugar which has been sifted twice. Add egg yolks, flour and flavoring. Bake in preheated oven (350° F) in an ungreased pan (9" x 13") for 40–45 minutes. Hang upside down to cool (invert, as for angel food cake). Cut in strips any size.

In a medium-sized bowl, mix butter with sugar and egg* until smooth (for icing). Makes 1½ cups of icing. Spread all sides of strips with the icing. Roll in peanuts. Makes about 36 (3-inch-long) pieces.

*Note: The egg used in the icing is not cooked. Eliminate it or use egg substitute instead. ✶

The First Lady preferred small, informal gatherings. Once a year she hosted a luncheon for her Spanish class. Professor Ramon and 12 of his students gathered in the White House kitchen to prepare a Cuban dish called "Picadillo."

Ramon instructed them in Spanish on how to cut the meat, mix it with rice and season it with hot spices. They sang Spanish songs and learned the names of different kitchen utensils. Mrs. Truman worked alongside Mrs. Dean Acheson, wife of the Undersecretary of State; Mrs. Leverett Saltonstall, whose husband was a senator from Massachusetts; and Mrs. Lester Pearson, wife of the Canadian Ambassador.

When the meal was ready, other classmates acted as waitresses. The women who put on the aprons included Mrs. Dwight Eisenhower; Mrs. Hugo Black, whose husband was a Supreme Court Justice; and the wives of the Secretary of War, the Assistant Secretary of the Navy and the head of the Reconstruction Finance Corporation.

They served the food to 66 fellow students, who were seated in the State Dining Room. After lunch, they gathered in the East Room for more Spanish songs. The event was a huge success, especially since the White House staff cleaned up all the dishes.

Mrs. Truman's
Bing Cherry Salad Mold

1 package lime Jell-O
8 ounces cream cheese
1 15-ounce can Bing cherries
1 package cherry Jell-O

Make lime Jell-O according to package directions. Let it set for 30 minutes. Beat cheese until soft. Add lime Jell-O and beat again. Put in bottom of mold; let set in refrigerator for 2–3 hours.

Measure juice from cherries. Add enough water to make 2 cups. Heat juice. Add cherry Jell-O and stir to dissolve. When cool, pour on top of lime Jell-O. Let set 30 minutes and then add cherries. Cool 2–3 hours in refrigerator until set. Invert onto plate and serve. ★

Truman Family Pound Cake

1 pound sugar (2 cups)
1 pound flour (4 cups)
¾ pound butter
1½ teaspoons lemon extract
9 egg yolks, beaten
9 egg whites, beaten

Preheat oven to 325° F. Combine first five ingredients and stir until thoroughly blended. (It is easier to cream butter and sugar first, then alternately add egg yolks and flour. Mix thoroughly.) Gently fold in egg whites. Bake in a buttered and floured tube pan for 1 hour or until cake springs back when pressed. Top with a white icing and nut halves.

This recipe has been in the Truman family for over 200 years. Mrs. Truman added this note on the bottom of the recipe, "I personally think it needs more butter!" ★

The Trumans' favorite cocktail was an "old-fashioned." No matter what he tried, the head butler, Alonzo Fields, could not seem to make the drink to their liking. Finally he simply poured bourbon over ice. The First Lady said, "Now that's the way we like our old-fashioneds!"

In 1952, Truman's doctor advised him to drink two shots of bourbon a day so he would live another 20 years. He followed the doctor's orders, and he passed away in 1972. Truman began his morning with a shot of bourbon and a large glass of orange juice.

Truman Family's Favorite Ozark Pudding

☆

Recipe from Vietta Carr
(The Family Cook)

1 egg
¾ cup sugar
1¼ teaspoons baking powder
3 heaping tablespoons flour
⅛ teaspoon salt
½ cup chopped apples
½ cup chopped nuts
1 teaspoon vanilla
1 cup heavy cream, whipped

Beat egg well and add sugar, beating until light and creamy. Sift flour, baking powder and salt, and add to egg mixture; blend well. Fold in apples and nuts; add vanilla. Pour into (an 8") greased paper-lined dish; bake in a slow oven (325° F) for 30 minutes. Serve with whipped cream. *

Harry and Bess focused a great deal of love and affection on their only daughter, Margaret. The family was so close that the White House staff nicknamed them "The Three Musketeers." The President referred to his wife as "The Boss" and called their daughter "The Boss's Boss."

Sometimes at dinner the family playfully threw bits of bread at each other or held watermelon seed-spitting contests.

"Within the first few months, I discovered that being a President is like riding a tiger. A man has to keep on riding or be swallowed."

—*Harry Truman*

Mrs. Truman's Turkey Stuffing ☆

10 slices dry bread
¼ pound butter
1 cup diced onions
1 cup diced celery
1 cup hot water, in which giblets have been
  cooked
Salt, pepper and poultry seasoning to taste

Dry out bread in a slow oven (275° F for 15–20 minutes). Cut into ½-inch cubes. Put butter in pan, add onions and celery and sauté until light brown. Add water and let simmer 5 minutes. Add bread cubes. Season with salt, pepper and poultry seasoning to taste.

Note: Dressing should be neither too wet nor too dry. It should be a semi-moist dressing so that when it is done it will be light and fluffy. This is an exceedingly fine dressing for chicken or turkey. For larger size birds, the amounts must be increased accordingly. ✶

During his presidency, Truman had a weeklong vacation in Key West, Florida, where he stayed in the empty Naval Commander's home. He fell in love with the place and returned 11 times.

The Little White House, as it became known, was used for vacations as well as working meetings. Among the guests were Vice President Alben Barkley, Speaker of the House Sam Rayburn and Chief Justice Fred Vinson.

Mrs. Vinson attended a picnic on the lawn and pointed out that in spite of all the security precautions, a coconut could simply fall out of a tree and hit the President on the head. The Secret Service had already thought of that—all the coconuts were wired to the trees.

"I never give them hell; I just tell them the truth and they think it is hell."

—*Harry Truman*

Truman's Favorite Buttermilk Pie

½ cup butter
2 cups sugar
3 eggs
3 tablespoons flour
¼ teaspoon salt
1 cup buttermilk
1 unbaked 9-inch pie shell
½ cup pecans, chopped

Cream butter. Add sugar, ½ cup at a time, beating after each addition. Add eggs, one at a time. Combine flour and salt, add to butter mixture a small amount at a time. Add buttermilk. Batter should look like a cake mix that needs more flour. Pour into pie shell. Bake at 300° F for 1½ hours or until golden brown. Sprinkle chopped pecans on top of pie. *

This recipe is from Chief Steward Harry T. Hightower. He was Truman's personal cook when they went to Rio de Janeiro on the battleship *Missouri* in 1947.

The President liked the pie so much that he sent an aide to find out how it was made. The recipe had been a secret in Hightower's family for a long time, and he just couldn't bring himself to give the recipe to the President. Upon Hightower's retirement from the Navy, he allowed the recipe to be published in the *Navy Times*.

During Truman's second term, the White House was found to be structurally unsound, and one architect said the house was standing purely out of habit. The historic exterior was left intact, but the mansion was completely gutted and rebuilt with steel beams. The renovations, which also included air-conditioning and a modern commercial kitchen, cost $5,761,000.

The project took three years, and during that time the Trumans lived across the street in the Blair-Lee House. They found the intimate setting of the house much more to their liking, and they entertained smaller groups there.

The President moved back into the Executive Mansion with only three months left in his term. Truman had the Lincoln bed and furniture moved into a room upstairs, and this became known as the Lincoln Bedroom.

"The White House is the finest prison in the world."

—*Harry Truman*

Dwight D. Eisenhower

№ 34

President Eisenhower's Chili con Carne

3 tablespoons bacon grease
6 to 8 medium-sized onions
1 large clove garlic
2 pounds lean ground chuck or round steak
2 tablespoons salt
2 ounces chili powder
1½ quarts water
2 to 3 cans red beans (not kidney beans)
1 heaping teaspoon comino seed, ground (cumin)

Put bacon grease in a large iron skillet or Dutch oven. Cut up the onions and garlic. When the bacon fat is heated, add the onions and garlic. Cook for about 10 minutes, stirring occasionally. Add the meat. When this has lost its red color, add salt and chili powder and stir well. Add water. Simmer for about an hour.

Add two or three cans of red beans, depending on your preference. Then add ground comino seed. Make a small mixture of flour and water (about 2 tablespoons of each) and add to the chili. This will take up any excess grease and improve its consistency.

It is recommended that the chili is cooked at least several hours before it is to be served, then reheated. Or better still, make it the day before and reheat it. ★

During their married life, Ike and Mamie lived in 28 homes. Their eight years in the White House was the longest period they resided in one place.

As an Army wife, Mamie had become accustomed to entertaining, and she was a charming hostess. One Frenchman told a friend, "Her smile anticipated the sunrise by almost an hour. She was radiant, monsieur, absolutely radiant."

Mrs. Eisenhower was not in the best of health, with a heart condition and an inner ear problem that affected her balance. This caused some people to wonder if she was tipsy, but she rarely drank alcoholic beverages. Even though she often rested until the last minute before a party, Mamie tired easily when standing at receptions, so a chair was close by so she could steady herself or sit down.

President Eisenhower's Old-Fashioned Big Party Beef Stew

20 pounds stewing meat (prime round)
3 gallons beef stock
8 pounds small Irish potatoes
6 bunches small carrots
5 pounds small onions
15 fresh tomatoes, chopped
1 bunch bouquet garniture
Salt, pepper and Ac'cent

Stew the meat in the beef stock until tender. Add vegetables and bouquet garniture.* Season with salt, pepper and Ac'cent to taste. Cover and cook until vegetables are done. Strain off 2 gallons of stock from stew and thicken slightly with beef roux.** Pour back into the stew and let simmer for ½ hour.

   *The bouquet garniture (or garni) is made up of thyme, bay leaves and garlic tied in a cheesecloth bag. This permits a mingling of the seasonings without any one of them dominating the stew. **The beef roux is 1½ pints of fat collected from the top of the marrow bone stock and mixed with a pound of flour. Serves 60. ★

☆ President Eisenhower's Old-Fashioned Family-Size Beef Stew

2½ cups beef stock
2 pounds stewing beef
Assorted spices (thyme, bay leaf, garlic, etc.)
1 bunch small carrots
¼ pound tomatoes
1 pound small potatoes
Salt and pepper to taste
2 tablespoons butter
2 tablespoons flour

Put beef stock into a large pot. Add stew meat and cook until tender. Put spices in a cheesecloth bag and add to pot. Chop the vegetables and potatoes and add to pot. Add salt and pepper to taste. Cook until potatoes are done.

   In a separate pan, melt butter. Add flour and blend well. Cook over low heat for 3–5 minutes, stirring constantly. Strain off 1 cup of stock and slowly add to flour mixture. Blend well and pour back into stew. Simmer until ready to serve (about ½ hour). Remove spice bag. Serves 6. ★

President Eisenhower's Potato Salad

(Retold by a Fishing Buddy)
Original Recipe

Boil potatoes, slice or cube and marinate in wine vinegar for 20 minutes. Drain and mix with chopped onions and chopped parsley. Salt and pepper to taste. Pour the used vinegar over this mixture and add mayonnaise to taste, spiked with ⅛ teaspoon of Worcestershire sauce, celery salt and a pinch of garlic salt. Serve cold, garnished with sliced hard-boiled eggs, sliced pimento and olives.

Approximate Quantities to Serve 12
3 to 4 pounds potatoes
½ cup red wine vinegar
1 onion, chopped
1 cup parsley, chopped
½ cup mayonnaise
½ teaspoon Worcestershire sauce
Pinch of celery salt
Pinch of garlic salt
Salt and pepper to taste
1 to 2 eggs, hard-boiled
Pimento for garnish
6 to 10 olives, chopped *

☆ Mamie's Million Dollar Fudge

12 ounces semisweet chocolate bits
12 ounces German sweet chocolate, broken into bits
1 pint marshmallow crème
Pinch of salt
1 can (12 to 13 ounces) evaporated milk
4½ cups sugar
2 cups chopped nut meats
2 tablespoons butter

In a large bowl, combine both types of chocolate, marshmallow crème and salt. Put milk and sugar in a large pot. Bring to a boil, stirring constantly. Cook (over medium-low heat), stirring continuously, for 6–7 minutes. Pour the milk mixture over the chocolate. Add nuts and butter and beat until the chocolate is melted and the fudge is creamy.

Pour into a buttered 9" x 13" pan and let cool at room temperature for a few hours before cutting into squares. Store in an airtight container. Makes about 5 pounds of fudge. *

This recipe got its name from President Eisenhower, who was very fond of the dessert. It is worth every calorie!

"I can make only two things: mayonnaise and fudge," said Mrs. Eisenhower, who did not consider herself to be a good cook. She also once said, "I was a cooking school dropout."

A talented amateur chef, President Eisenhower enjoyed grilling and often barbecued on the roof of the White House. He began cooking as a boy, when his younger brother Milton got scarlet fever. Half the family, including their mother, was quarantined upstairs. Ike was put in charge of the meals, with his mother calling directions down the stairs.

He later said, "... cooking gave me a creative feeling. I don't think the family lived too well during those weeks, but I learned something about the preparation of simple dishes for the table."

As a general during World War II, Eisenhower continued his interest in food—even on the front line. He thought the Army rations tasted much better if they were hot. When he was driven anywhere, he devised a way to keep the food tins on the hood of the jeep. The heat from the engine warmed up the food, and by the time they reached their destination, the food was nice and hot.

Squirrel Stew with Leftovers ☆

3 squirrels, skinned and cleaned
2 onions, peeled and chopped
3 ribs celery, if available
Few sprigs parsley, if available
2 teaspoons salt
Pepper to taste
2 gallons water
Leftover potatoes
Leftover beans

Place squirrels, onion, chopped celery, chopped parsley, salt and pepper in a large pot with the water. Bring to a boil. Reduce heat and simmer until water is reduced to about 1½ quarts. Remove squirrels, bone, and cut meat into bite-size pieces. Return meat to pot along with leftover potatoes and beans. Serve with lots of bread and butter. ✱

"Oh, that lovely title, ex-president."
—*Dwight D. Eisenhower*

As a boy, Eisenhower enjoyed camping with his friends in the woods. On one trip, they ran out of food, so he and a friend set out hunting in the forest. They caught three squirrels, and Eisenhower made squirrel stew, then he and his buddy pretended that the meat was from a crow. No one else wanted the stew, so Eisenhower and his pal ate the entire meal.

Later in his life, he wasn't quite so fond of squirrels. An avid golfer, Eisenhower had a putting green put on the White House lawn ... and squirrels buried acorns in the middle of the green. The President ordered the critters banished, so they were caught and then released in Rock Creek Park.

One friend teased him for spending so much time on the golf course and suggested they establish a fund to protect the squirrels from Ike's wayward balls.

Eisenhower is reportedly the only President to have scored a hole in one. But he could be a sore loser ... he nearly broke someone's shin because he threw his golf club. After he left office, Eisenhower wondered why he didn't win as many golf games as he did when he was President.

Mamie's Deep Dish Apple Pie ☆

6 tart apples
½ cup sugar
½ cup brown sugar
½ teaspoon nutmeg
Grated rind of 1 lemon
Grated rind of 1 orange
3 tablespoons butter or oleomargarine
Half of the pastry recipe (below)

Pare and core apples; cut into eighths. Place in a deep, greased baking dish. Combine sugar, brown sugar, nutmeg, lemon rind and orange rind. Sprinkle over apples. Dot with butter or oleomargarine. Top with a thin sheet of pastry, pricked in a design. Bake in a hot oven (425° F for about 30 minutes). Serves 6.

Pastry
2 cups flour
¾ teaspoon salt
⅔ cup shortening
Cold water

Sift flour; measure. Mix and sift flour and salt. Cut in shortening with two knives or pastry blender until flour shortening particles are about the size of small peas. Sprinkle 1 tablespoon of cold water over mixture and mix in lightly with a fork. Continue adding water in this fashion until pastry gathers around fork in a soft ball. Divide pastry in half and roll each half separately on lightly floured board to ⅛-inch thickness. Handle rolling pin very lightly. Makes enough for two 9-inch pie crusts.

Note: Make half of this recipe for the Deep Dish Apple Pie recipe (above) or other one-crust pies. ✻

Mrs. Eisenhower liked things done quickly and with military precision. The house was to be kept sparkling clean. Chief Usher West remembers, "She could give orders, staccato, crisp, detailed and final, as if it were she who had been a five-star general."

After informal dinners, Mamie often played the electric organ while guests sang along.

The family enjoyed spending weekends at the presidential retreat in Maryland. Originally used by President Franklin Roosevelt, the hideaway had been called Shangri-la. The house was a hodgepodge design, resulting from three cabins being put together. Mamie had the house renovated, and the retreat was renamed Camp David, after the Eisenhowers' grandson. The President confessed that Shangri-la was "just a little too fancy for a Kansas farm boy."

John F. Kennedy

№ 35

President Kennedy's Favorite Fish Chowder

2 pounds haddock
2 ounces salt pork, diced
2 onions, sliced
4 large potatoes, diced
1 cup chopped celery
1 bay leaf, crumbled
1 teaspoon salt
Freshly ground black pepper
1 quart milk
2 tablespoons butter

Place haddock in a large pot. Add 2 cups of water and bring to a boil. Reduce heat and simmer 15 minutes. Drain off the liquid, reserving it for later. Remove bones from fish and discard. Sauté salt pork until crisp and set aside. Add onions to pot and sauté until golden brown. Add fish, potatoes, celery, bay leaf, salt and pepper.

Add enough water to fish broth to make 3 cups of liquid. Add to pot. Bring to a boil, then reduce heat and simmer, uncovered, for 30 minutes. Add milk and butter and simmer 5 minutes. Serve chowder sprinkled with diced salt pork. Serves 6. ✷

On the campaign trail, Kennedy didn't have time for regular meals, so he carried a thermos of this fish chowder, a Kennedy clan favorite. The President also loved Boston clam chowder.

When the Prime Minister of Canada, Lester Pearson, visited Kennedy in Hyannisport, he and the President requested that the chef make the same chowder three days in a row.

The word "chowder" comes from the French *chaudiére*, which was the name of the huge copper pot used in fishing villages. When fishermen returned from the sea, they would put part of their catch in the community pot.

"I think 'Hail to the Chief' has a nice ring to it."
—*John F. Kennedy*

Directions for Making a CHOUDER

First lay some Onions to keep the Pork from burning,
Because in Chouder there can be no turning;
Then lay some Pork in slices very thin,
Thus you in Chouder always must begin.
Next lay some Fish, cut crossways very nice
Then season well with Pepper, Salt and Spice;
Parsley, Sweet-Marjoram, Savory and Thyme,
Then Biscuit next which must be soak'd some Time,
Thus your Foundation laid, you will be able
To raise a Chouder, high as Tower of Babel;
For by repeating o're the same again,
You may make Chouder for a thousand Men,
Last Bottle of Claret, with Water eno' to smother 'em,
You'll have a Mess which some call Omnium gather 'em.

Earliest American recipe for
chowder, 1751

The night before Kennedy's inauguration, a tremendous snowstorm immobilized Washington. Fortunately the storm abated by the next morning, and the sun shone on the proceedings. However, the temperature was so cold that the reporters' ballpoint pens froze, and they were forced to use pencils.

The lunch following the ceremony featured stuffed lobster, cream of tomato soup with crushed popcorn, and *patisserie bateau blanche.*

☆ Mrs. Kennedy's Beef Stroganoff

2 pounds boneless beef sirloin
Salt and pepper to taste
3 tablespoons flour
4 tablespoons butter, divided
2 cups beef broth
½ cup sour cream
3 teaspoons tomato juice or paste

Cut the beef into strips and season generously with salt and pepper. Cover and let stand for 2 hours in a cool place (refrigerator). In a large skillet, whisk flour and 3 tablespoons of butter over low heat until mixture bubbles and forms a smooth paste. Slowly add beef broth, stirring constantly until mixture thickens. Let boil 2 minutes.

Reduce heat and add sour cream alternately with tomato juice, still whisking. Simmer 1 minute; do not let it boil. In a separate pan, brown beef in remaining butter over medium heat. Add meat to the sauce. Season with salt and pepper. Simmer gently, or cook over hot water in double boiler, for 20 minutes. Serves 6. ★

President Kennedy's Favorite Waffles

¼ cup butter
1 tablespoon sugar
2 eggs, separated
1 cup plus 1 tablespoon sifted cake flour
⅞ cup milk or 1 cup buttermilk
Pinch of salt
4 teaspoons baking powder

Cream butter and sugar. Beat in egg yolks. Add flour and milk alternately. When ready to bake, fold in stiffly beaten egg whites, and add baking powder (and salt). Mixture should be thick and fluffy. Pour about ¼ of batter onto waffle iron and cook until light brown. Repeat. Serve with hot maple syrup and melted butter. Yields 4–5 waffles. ★

"Mothers all want their sons to grow up to be President, but they don't want them to become politicians in the process."

—John F. Kennedy

JFK's administration was filled with vitality and the laughter of his and Jacqueline's young children. Four-year-old Caroline would sit at the top of the stairs in her pink pajamas to watch the great parties below. At one outdoor ceremony, little John sailed a toy airplane from the balcony and hit a soldier directly on the head.

A schoolroom for Caroline was established in the top-floor solarium of the White House, and a playground was added outdoors. Caroline had pet ducks that often waddled across the lawn. The children also had a dog and a pet pony named "Macaroni" that Caroline loved to ride.

Mrs. Kennedy was a very involved parent who did not hesitate to discipline her children. "Whatever else you do, unless you raise your children well, I think you have failed," she said.

Jackie tried to shield them from the press, but when she was away, the President brought the children into the Oval Office for photo opportunities. Caroline was once photographed tottering into a press conference wearing her mother's high heels, and an image was captured of John Jr. waving good-bye as his father took off in a helicopter.

Mrs. Kennedy's Crème Brûlée ☆

3 cups heavy cream
1-inch piece of vanilla bean
6 tablespoons white sugar
6 egg yolks
½ cup brown sugar

In the top of double boiler, heat cream with vanilla bean. In a separate bowl, beat white sugar with egg yolks until creamy. Take out vanilla bean, and stir the warm cream into the yolks very carefully and slowly. Return the mixture to the double boiler, over boiling water. Stir constantly until the custard coats the spoon. Then put into a glass serving dish and place it in the refrigerator to set.

When ready to serve, cover the top of the custard with the brown sugar. Place the serving dish in a tray of crushed ice and place custard under the broiler flame until the sugar melts and caramelizes. Keep watching it or the sugar will burn. Serve immediately. Serves 6. ★

"I'm sick and tired of starring in everybody's home movies."

—*Jacqueline Kennedy*

The President enjoyed living in the White House, but Mrs. Kennedy resented the invasion of her privacy, saying, "I felt as if I had just turned into a piece of public property."

She only wanted her close friends to call her "Jackie", but soon the nation referred to her by that nickname. Mrs. Kennedy also disliked the term "First Lady." She said, "It sounds like a saddle horse."

Many social changes were introduced by the Kennedys. Receiving lines were eliminated so they could mingle freely with their guests. The number of dinner courses was cut to four—a soup or fish course, the main entrée, salad and dessert.

After dinner, the men mixed with the ladies instead of going to separate rooms. Urns of cigarettes were placed on the table, and ashtrays and matches were put at every place. Fires were lit in the fireplaces, and fresh natural-looking flower arrangements were put in antique pitchers.

Mrs. Kennedy chose dinner menus carefully, keeping in mind the tastes and customs of visitors. The President often went over the guest list for events and usually stopped to taste the wine before dressing for dinner. His favorite drink was beer while Mrs. Kennedy liked daiquiris.

One memorable State Dinner was held for Ayub Khan, the President of Pakistan. The guests traveled down the Potomac River on the presidential yacht trailed by PT boats (alluding to JFK's heroic service in WWII).

When they arrived at Mount Vernon, guests were offered mint juleps made from a recipe attributed to President George Washington (see recipe on page 17). Guests were able to tour the historic house, which was lit entirely by candles. There was a parade of the Fife and Drum Corps, dressed in Colonial costumes. Dinner was served under a tent decorated by Tiffany.

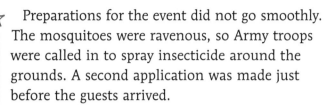

Preparations for the event did not go smoothly. The mosquitoes were ravenous, so Army troops were called in to spray insecticide around the grounds. A second application was made just before the guests arrived.

The National Symphony Orchestra was scheduled to play, but during the afternoon rehearsal, it was impossible for them to be heard. An acoustical shell was hastily erected to project the sound. The food was prepared at the White House and transported 12 miles to Mount Vernon. The military vehicles that carried the food also served as field kitchens.

The guests were unaware of the near disasters, and they sailed back up the river with memories of a magical evening.

Menu for the State Dinner in Honor of the President of Pakistan July 11, 1961

Avocado and Crabmeat Mimosa
Haut-Brion Blanc 1958
Poulet Chasseur
Couronne de Riz Clamart
Moet et Chandon Imperial Brut 1955
Framboises à la Crème Chantilly
Petits Fours Sec
Demitasse and Liqueurs

Soufflé Froid au Chocolat

Attributed to Mrs. Kennedy

2 1-ounce squares unsweetened chocolate
½ cup powdered sugar
1 cup milk
1 envelope unflavored gelatin
3 tablespoons cold water
¾ cup granulated sugar
1 teaspoon vanilla extract
¼ teaspoon salt
2 cups heavy cream

Put chocolate in top of double boiler. Melt over hot, not boiling, water. Stir in powdered sugar. Heat milk just until a thin film shows on the surface, then slowly add to chocolate and mix well. Remove from double boiler and place on low heat. Stir constantly until just before mixture reaches the boiling point. Remove from stove.

Soften gelatin in cold water for 3–5 minutes. Then stir into chocolate. Add granulated sugar, vanilla and salt. Put in refrigerator until slightly thickened. Remove from refrigerator and whip until light and fluffy. Whip cream until it holds a shape, then fold it into the chocolate. Pour into 2-quart mold or serving dish. Chill 2–3 hours or until ready to serve. Serves 6–8. ★

JFK appreciated fine food, but he enjoyed the basics as well, like chowder and baked beans. He was conscience of nutrition, and a bowl of grapes or apples was kept handy for snacks, but he also had a sweet tooth and loved whipped cream and angel food cake.

The President was an enthusiastic swimmer and often used the indoor pool at the White House. His father, Ambassador Joseph Kennedy, commissioned a mural for the walls featuring a scene with colorful sailboats. The President held swim races with members of his Cabinet. He often swam in the nude, and sometimes he raced his Welsh terrier, "Charlie."

Lyndon B. Johnson

№ 36

President Johnson's Pedernales River Chili

4 pounds ground beef
1 large onion, chopped
2 cloves garlic, minced
1 teaspoon oregano
1 teaspoon comino seed (cumin)
6 teaspoons chili powder, or more if needed
1½ cups canned tomatoes
Salt to taste
2 cups hot water

Put meat, onion and garlic in a large heavy skillet. Sear until light colored. Add oregano, comino seed, chili powder, tomatoes, salt and hot water. Bring to a boil. Lower heat and simmer about 1 hour. Skim off fat as it cooks out. Serves 8. ★

When the Johnsons moved into the White House, there wasn't enough matching china to use at large banquets. The first State Dinner was served on a combination of china from the Truman, Eisenhower and FDR administrations.

Mrs. Johnson worked with Tiffany and Co. to create a service featuring American wildflowers. Forty different flowers are featured on the china, with the dessert plates showing the official flowers of the 50 states.

State Dinners usually required guests to dress in white tie and tails. Johnson disliked this formality, so during his administration, most important functions were black tie. Johnson may have been the best dancer of all the Presidents. Jackie Kennedy called him "my favorite dance partner." His daughter Luci also enjoyed dancing and was nicknamed "Watusi Luci."

"Don't do anything you wouldn't mind seeing on the front page of the newspaper." (Advice she gave to her daughter.)

—*Lady Bird Johnson*

President Johnson's Chinese Chop Suey

½ pound lean pork or chicken
2 tablespoons fat
1 cup diced celery
¾ cup diced onions
1 cup bouillon
¼ cup mushrooms
1 tablespoon cornstarch
2 tablespoons water
1 #2½ can bean sprouts, drained*
1 #2½ can mixed vegetables*
1 teaspoon salt
¼ teaspoon sugar
Dash of white pepper
Dash of paprika
More than a dash of garlic powder
Rice and crisp noodles
2 tablespoons soy sauce (optional)

Cut meat into small pieces, and brown in fat. Add celery, onions and bouillon; cover and simmer for 20 minutes. Add mushrooms and a paste made of cornstarch and water, and cook for 10 minutes, stirring until thickened. Add bean sprouts, mixed vegetables and seasonings, and heat thoroughly.

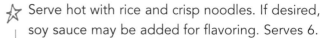 Serve hot with rice and crisp noodles. If desired, soy sauce may be added for flavoring. Serves 6.
   *A #2½ can is equal to 27–29 ounces, or about 3½ cups. ★

Lyndon and Lady Bird were outgoing and gregarious. Dinners at the White House were more informal, and many innovative types of entertaining were begun. For the first time, a State Dinner was hosted in the Rose Garden.

The staff made two sets of plans for the event, in case of inclement weather. The evening sky was clear, however, and as the moon rose, it cast a magical glow over the garden. Japanese lanterns glowed over the tables, and the Marine Band played from one end of the terrace.

Coffee and liqueurs were served indoors. Guests then returned outside and were treated to music by the National Symphony Orchestra and a performance by two principle dancers from the New York City Ballet.

At first Mrs. Johnson felt intimidated about living in the historic house. "It's hard to feel at home in a house that belongs to 180 million people. I sometimes hear history thundering down the corridors," she remarked. "For about 2 weeks I sort of tiptoed and whispered—but now the day's work stretches out in front of me each morning and I don't tiptoe anymore."

Mrs. Johnson's Cheese Wafers ☆

1 cup margarine or soft butter
2 cups flour
3 ounces sharp cheddar cheese, grated
1 teaspoon cayenne pepper
½ teaspoon salt
2 cups Rice Krispies cereal

Cut butter into flour, add cheese and seasonings. Fold in cereal. Drop by small rounds on ungreased cookie sheet and flatten with a spoon. Bake at 350° F for about 12–15 minutes, depending on oven (careful not to get too brown). Yields approximately 5 dozen wafers. ★

Mrs. Johnson's Nachos Special

8 tortillas
Fat for frying
½ pound cheese
Jalapeños (hot peppers)

Cut tortillas into quarters and fry in deep hot fat until brown and crisp on both sides. Drain well. Place about 1 teaspoon of grated cheese on each quarter and top with a slice of jalapeño pepper. Put in hot oven (450° F) until well heated and cheese begins to melt. Serve at once. Serves 16. ★

LBJ loved most types of food, but he was especially fond of Mexican dishes. There was a saying in the White House kitchen that the President "will eat anything that doesn't bite him first."

He wanted to be kept in touch at all times, so he had a telephone installed in his bathroom and another one on a leg of the family dining table.

Johnson liked to have his salad chopped so finely that he could eat it with a spoon. That way he could race through his meal and get on to other things.

Mrs. Johnson allowed the staff to oversee the daily routine of the White House, preferring to spend her time on other things. She took on several environmental causes, including a highway beautification project to rid America's roads of unsightly billboards. Lady Bird also promoted the cultivation of the country's native wildflowers and trees.

"If one morning I walked on top of the water across the Potomac River, the headline that afternoon would read: 'President can't swim.'"
—Lyndon B. Johnson

President Johnson's Barbecue Sauce

1 clove garlic
¼ cup butter or margarine
¼ vinegar
¼ cup catsup
¼ cup lemon juice
¼ cup Worcestershire sauce
½ teaspoon salt
⅛ teaspoon black pepper
⅛ teaspoon red pepper
2 drops hot sauce

Sauté garlic in butter in a small saucepan over low heat 5 minutes. Add remaining ingredients; stir well. Bring mixture to a boil; reduce heat and simmer 20 minutes. Use sauce for barbecuing beef, pork or chicken. Yields ¾ cup. ★

It was said that you couldn't understand LBJ until you understood his barbecues. His chief of staff said politics and barbecue just went together in Texas, why not Washington?

Parties were held on Johnson's 2,718-acre ranch and were used as a diplomatic tool to bring people together. He sometimes gave visitors a tour of the ranch by driving 90 miles an hour around the property.

Johnson was the first President to hold a barbecue at the White House. He hired Walter Jetton, "barbecue king" from Texas, to organize the event. A giant pit was dug in the lawn, and ribs were charbroiled over the fire. The sauce was served on the side, so guests could dip the ribs in it if they wished.

Mrs. Johnson's Spinach Parmesan

3 pounds (fresh) spinach, cleaned
6 tablespoons grated Parmesan cheese
6 tablespoons minced onion
6 tablespoons heavy cream
5 tablespoons melted butter
½ cup cracker crumbs

Cook spinach until tender. Drain thoroughly and add the cheese, onion, cream and 4 tablespoons of the butter. Arrange in a shallow 1-quart baking dish, and sprinkle with the crumbs mixed with the remaining butter. Bake for 10–15 minutes at 375° F. Serves 8. ★

President Johnson was very social, but he liked to mix politics and pleasure. He would dance with a congressman's wife and tell her to get her husband to go along with him on a particular bill.

LBJ would socialize until late at night. His social secretary said, "He would stay so late that we had to pass the word to people that it wouldn't be counted rude if they slipped away before the President."

Sometimes a menu was modified to name a dish after an honored guest. "Glacé Imelda" was a pineapple-lime sherbet dessert served to President and Mrs. Marcos. The same dessert was renamed "Glacé Inonu" for the visit of Prime Minister Ismet Inonu of Turkey.

The Johnsons hosted a special luncheon for former First Lady Mamie Eisenhower. Several tables were set up in the State Dining Room, and each one featured china from a different administration. The menu consisted of foods named after Presidents: Monroe's Quaking Jelly, LBJ's Minced Ham Turnovers, Jefferson's Filled Pannequaiques, Bouquet of Garden Vegetables à la John Adams and Andrew Jackson's Burnt Cream.

LBJ Ranch Spiced Tea

8 cups boiling water
4 family-size tea bags
1 6-ounce can frozen limeade
1 6-ounce can frozen orange juice
1 stick cinnamon
A few whole cloves
Sugar to taste

Place all ingredients in a large pot and simmer a few minutes. Remove tea bags, cinnamon and cloves. This tea may be served hot or cold. ★

This is a favorite of family and guests at the ranch, in summer or winter.

The top-floor solarium was turned into a hangout for the Johnsons' daughters, Luci and Lynda. This was a private area with no Secret Service, and the girls held parties here. Luci redecorated the area to include a television, record player and soda bar. The tile floor was perfect for dancing, and the comfortable couches were a good place to bring a date.

On her first night in the White House, Luci and a friend decided to light a fire in her bedroom fireplace. They forgot to open the chimney flue, and the room filled with smoke. Luci stood on the desk in her nightgown and tried to open the window, "and there was a White House policeman looking straight at me."

The girls tried unsuccessfully to put out the fire with glasses of water, but fortunately a White House attendant soon rushed in and opened the damper. Luci later said, "I spent my first week in the White House getting rid of the smoke on my newly painted walls. It was my first night in the White House, and I was going to burn the place down!"

Both of the Johnson daughters were married during his term in office. Lynda Bird was married in a private ceremony in the East Room. Luci Baines was married at the National Shrine of the Immaculate Conception, but both wedding receptions were held in the White House.

☆ LBJ Ranch Hush Puppies

2 cups white cornmeal
3 tablespoons sugar
1 tablespoon salt
1 teaspoon baking powder
3½ cups boiling water
¼ cup butter

Over heat, combine cornmeal, sugar, salt and baking powder. Slowly add boiling water, stirring briskly. As soon as mixture is smooth, remove from the heat and stir in butter. Cool. Shape into "fingers" and fry in 2 inches hot fat (375° F) until golden brown. Drain on absorbent paper. Makes about 3 dozen hush puppies. ✳

LBJ was an avid big game hunter, and he loved to hunt deer on his ranch in Texas. He often snacked on biscuits stuffed with venison sausage. He gave packages of the sausage to staff and Cabinet members at Christmastime.

Richard Nixon

№️ 37

Mrs. Nixon's
Fillet de Boeuf Wellington

5 pounds beef fillet
4 ounces melted butter
Salt and pepper to taste
½ cup chopped celery
½ cup chopped onion
1 tablespoon chopped parsley
1 bay leaf
8 ounces pâté de foie gras
11 to 12 ounces pastry dough
2 egg yolks
4 tablespoons water

Preheat oven to 450° F. Trim fat from fillet. Brush well with butter, and sprinkle with salt and pepper. Roast about 25 minutes in flat pan with celery, onion, parsley and bay leaf. Remove from pan.

When fillet is cold, spread it with pâté de foie gras and wrap it in pastry rolled ⅛ inch thick. Bring pastry over fillet, moisten edges and press firmly to seal. Beat egg yolks and water together. Brush over pastry. Put on baking sheet. Bake at 450° F for about 15 minutes or until golden brown. ★

The election of Richard Nixon signaled a return to formal entertaining at the White House. Events were dignified and low-key. White tie and tails were required for formal occasions.

The President rarely danced at parties. Viewing social affairs as a time to conduct business, he usually seated the guest of honor to his right so they could discuss important issues.

When her husband was Vice President, Mrs. Nixon appeared somewhat stiff and uncomfortable in front of the public. She became accustomed to her role as hostess, and when she became First Lady, people described her as warm, kind and spontaneous. *Newsday* reported, "Pat Nixon has suddenly emerged from an icy cocoon of literal anonymity and proven herself a living, breathing, thinking, loving woman."

"You can't depend on the man who made the mess to clean it up."

—*Richard Nixon*

Mrs. Nixon's Shrimp Superb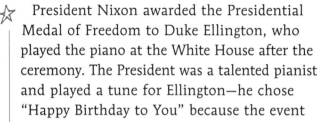

17 eggs, hard-boiled
1½ pounds raw shrimp or 1 pound frozen shrimp
6 ounces bleu cheese, crumbled
½ cup mayonnaise
¼ pound grated cheese (cheddar)
2 tablespoons honey
4 ounces potato chips

Shell the eggs. Shell and devein shrimp; simmer 2–5 minutes in boiling salted water to cover, or until pink and tender. Start heating oven to 250° F. Cut eggs into eighths and halve shrimp lengthwise. Put into a large bowl with bleu cheese, mayonnaise, cheese and honey. Mix well and turn into a 2-quart casserole dish. Crush potato chips; sprinkle over shrimp mixture. Bake 1 hour. Makes 15–20 appetizer or buffet servings. *

During Nixon's first year in office, over 50,000 guests came to the White House. Pat was an experienced hostess and accompanied him to China and Russia. When Nixon opened up relations with China, many Americans, including the First Family, developed a love of Chinese food.

They also liked simpler foods such as spaghetti, lasagna, Irish stew and beef enchiladas. The President especially liked steak and ordered his cooked medium-rare.

President Nixon awarded the Presidential Medal of Freedom to Duke Ellington, who played the piano at the White House after the ceremony. The President was a talented pianist and played a tune for Ellington—he chose "Happy Birthday to You" because the event happened to fall on Ellington's birthday.

One of the only State Dinners held outside the White House took place at the Hotel del Coronado in San Diego, California. Honoring Mexican President Gustavo Diaz Ordaz, the dinner featured Prime Sirloin Mexicana, California Roasted Potatoes and Colossal Asparagus Salad. Six hundred people attended, including former President Lyndon Johnson, California Governor Ronald Reagan, Frank Sinatra and John Wayne.

One of the most memorable parties held during the Nixon administration was a seated dinner for released prisoners of war. Tents were set up on the South Lawn, and the biggest one measured 100 x 180 feet—longer than the White House. A hundred extra waiters were hired to serve everyone.

Head chef Henry Haller recalled, "... the kitchen borrowed china, crystal and silver from a local caterer. We also 'borrowed' the Pentagon, where 90 quarts of strawberries were puréed in a giant blender, and the Washington Hotel, where 1,300 pounds of beef were roasted. Everyone seemed eager to help us honor the brave prisoners of war with a memorable White House party."

Mrs. Nixon's Potato Chip Salad ☆

4 cups chopped cooked chicken
2 cups chopped celery
1 cup grated cheese
⅔ cup mayonnaise (more to taste)
2 tablespoons onion
2 pimientos, chopped
½ tablespoon salt
1½ cups crushed potato chips
4 hard-boiled eggs

Combine all ingredients except potato chips and eggs. Add chips just before serving. Slice the eggs and use for decoration.

This unusual salad uses crushed potato chips to add a slightly crunchy texture. Once the potato chips have been added, the salad will not stay fresh for more than an hour. ⋆

The President occasionally helped out in the kitchen. His mother, Hannah Milhous Nixon, once said, "He was the best potato masher one could wish for. Even in these days, when I am visiting Richard and Pat in Washington, or when they visit me, he will take over the potato mashing. My feeling is that he actually enjoys it."

On their first day in the White House, Nixon requested some cottage cheese, and his daughter Tricia asked for a hot dog. The kitchen didn't have these items in stock, so the staff had to go scrambling to a nearby deli. After that, those foods were always kept in the White House kitchen.

Tricia Nixon's wedding to Edward Finch Cox took place in the Rose Garden on June 12, 1971. The menu included smoked salmon, roast beef, Alaska king crab, crêpes fondue Gruyère and coconut shrimp. The wedding cake, which was 5 feet wide and 7 feet tall, was dubbed "Washington's Newest Monument" by the press.

Mrs. Nixon's Meat Loaf

1½ pounds lean ground beef
3 tablespoons bread crumbs
2 tablespoons whipping cream
2 tablespoons tomato sauce
1 egg
1 tablespoon chopped parsley
2 teaspoons salt
¼ teaspoon black pepper, ground
1 teaspoon seasoning salt

Mix all ingredients well with meat; form loaf. Place loaf in a pan, cover top with additional tomato sauce (spread very thin over loaf). Bake 30 minutes at 375° F, then turn oven down to 350° F and bake 20 minutes more. Serves 6. ★

President Nixon's Favorite Country Omelet

1 medium-size potato
1 medium-size yellow onion
5 tablespoons butter
16 "dollar-size" pieces Virginia ham, ⅛ inch thick
8 eggs, beaten
Salt and pepper to taste

Thinly slice the potato and onion. Sauté sliced potato in hot butter until just done. Add onion and quickly cook until golden. Add ham and quickly cook until crisp. Add all to 10-inch omelet skillet with 4 tablespoons hot butter.

Add half of beaten eggs; let eggs set on bottom, holding vegetables and ham; add salt, pepper and rest of eggs. Cook, tilting pan to side, pushing in sides of omelet with spatula to let eggs run under and set on bottom. Set top under hot broiler. Serve warm or cold, in wedges. Serves 6–8. ★

Sunday night suppers often featured a country omelet or western-style omelet. The President also enjoyed a Spanish omelet, which has poached eggs and a spicy tomato sauce. Family dinners were served promptly at 6 p.m. They usually skipped the first course and rarely ate desserts unless there was company.

There was an unused herbarium on the third floor of the White House. Nixon had it renovated, and it was used to grow some of his favorite herbs—tarragon, chives, thyme and parsley.

Nixon was the first President to hold Sunday religious services in the East Room. After the service, everyone was invited to join them for breakfast.

Nixon loved to watch football, and Washington Redskins coach George Allen was a frequent guest at the White House.

Gerald R. Ford

№ 38

Mrs. Ford's Curry of Lamb with Rice

2 pounds lamb shoulder
3 tablespoons oil
1 tablespoon chopped onion
½ cup chopped celery
1 tablespoon curry powder
2 tablespoons minced parsley
1 tablespoon chopped pimiento
1 tablespoon flour
½ cup hot water
1 teaspoon salt

Remove the gristle and fat from the lamb. Cut meat into 1-inch cubes. Heat the oil with chopped onion and brown the meat. To the chopped celery add curry powder, parsley, pimiento and flour. Mix well with meat. Add hot water to which salt has been added. Cover and simmer 45 minutes to an hour, stirring frequently. Serve with steamed long-grain rice. Serves 4. ★

Gerald Ford enjoyed living in the White House and once joked it was "the best public housing I've ever seen." Betty arranged the family living quarters with comfortable furniture, and the President's favorite leather lounge chair was put in the den.

The family preferred hearty and wholesome meals, which were referred to as "Michigan Gourmet." Some of the President's favorite foods were pot roast, fish and liver with bacon. Sunday morning brunch featured waffles "with the works"—strawberries and sour cream.

"He just loves food," said Mrs. Ford. "All kinds of food. I have to take the plate away or he'll eat that, too."

Ford was one of the most athletic Presidents since Theodore Roosevelt. He liked to get up earlier than everyone else. Calisthenics and weight lifting were a regular part of his morning routine, and he often swam laps in the pool before dinner. The indoor pool built for Franklin Roosevelt had been filled in and converted into a pressroom by President Nixon. Ford had an outdoor pool built with donated funds. He said, "Fifteen minutes in the pool is worth two martinis."

Mrs. Ford's Carrot Vichyssoise ☆ Mrs. Ford's Chinese Pepper Steak

2 cups peeled and diced potatoes
1½ cups peeled and sliced carrots
3 cups canned chicken broth
1 tablespoon chopped onion
Salt and white pepper to taste
1 cup sour cream
1 heaping teaspoon chopped chives
Parsley for garnish

Simmer potatoes and carrots in chicken broth, and cook until soft, about 15–20 minutes. Add onion, salt and pepper. Remove from heat and cool 10 minutes. Pour into blender and purée until smooth. Cool in blender and chill thoroughly in refrigerator. Approximately 1 hour before serving, fold in sour cream and chopped chives. Serve with a topping of chopped parsley. Serves 6. *

Mrs. Ford kept an eye on the White House food budget and tried to make sure nothing went to waste ... so leftovers usually found their way into some sort of soup.

Other than at official functions, the President rarely ate desserts. An exception was butter pecan ice cream, which he never tired of. If he needed to lose weight, he ate cottage cheese, yogurt, salads or fruit. After a large State Dinner, the President ate very light meals the next day.

2 pounds flank steak
2 tablespoons shortening
3 green peppers, cut into 1½-inch pieces
1 package onion soup mix
2 tablespoons soy sauce
½ cup sherry
2 tablespoons cornstarch
½ teaspoon salt
⅛ teaspoon pepper

Cut steak lengthwise into ½-inch strips and then into 1-inch pieces. Melt shortening in a skillet and fry steak in several batches, just long enough for it to change color. Remove meat and sauté the green pepper.

Bring 2 cups water to a boil in a large pot. Add onion soup mix and continue to boil for 10 minutes. Stir in the meat and green pepper and simmer for 30 minutes. Add the soy sauce, sherry, cornstarch (diluted in a little water), salt and pepper. Cook until slightly thickened. For variation, add a can of bean sprouts and a little more cornstarch. Serve over steamed rice. Serves 4. *

Betty Ford liked to serve this dish on Valentine's Day.

Mrs. Ford's Homemade Toasting Bread

2 cups milk
½ cup white stone-ground cornmeal
2 teaspoons salt
1 tablespoon sugar
¼ cup shortening
1 package active dry yeast
¼ cup warm water
6 to 6½ cups sifted bread flour, preferably a high-protein, high-gluten variety

1. Heat 1 cup milk. Combine with cornmeal in a large mixing bowl. Cover the bowl and let rest overnight in a warm place.
2. In a small saucepan, heat remaining milk over medium heat until hot. Add to the cornmeal mixture with salt, sugar and shortening.
3. Mix yeast with warm water; stir into cornmeal mixture, using a wire whisk.
4. Add flour, 1 cup at a time, working first with a spoon, then by hand to achieve a smooth, elastic dough. (This will take about 5 minutes.) Turn out onto a lightly floured board.
5. Knead dough by hand, working outside edges in, for 5 minutes, in order to incorporate air into the dough. Return to the bowl.
6. Cover the bowl with a hot damp cloth and place in a warm spot for about 2 hours, or until doubled in bulk.
7. Turn out onto floured board; knead again, adding enough flour to make a smooth dough that does not stick to the board.
8. Use a sharp knife to divide dough into 2 equal loaves, and place each in a greased 9" x 5" loaf pan.
9. Cover with a hot damp cloth and let rise for 45 minutes, or until dough rises to a level even with the rims of the pans.
10. Preheat oven to 350° F.
11. Brush tops of loaves lightly with water. Use a long thin knife to slit tops down the middle; make each slit ¼ inch deep.
12. Bake on lower shelf of preheated oven for 40 minutes, or until golden brown and firm to the touch.
13. Turn loaves out onto wire racks; let cool completely before slicing. This bread tastes best toasted, and freezes well when wrapped tightly in plastic.

Yields 2 loaves.

Recipe from *The White House Family Cookbook* by Henry Haller, with Virginia Aronson, ©1987 by Henry Haller and Virginia Aronson. Used by permission of Random House, Inc. ★

The President wasn't fussy about meals. He often helped with the dishes and usually made his own breakfast—an English muffin, orange juice and grapefruit or melon. "All he needs is a toaster," said Betty.

Mrs. Ford's friendly and natural manner made her a very popular First Lady. She took a personal interest in working on the menus, and for table decorations she sometimes showcased American handicrafts by using items such as antique dolls or weather vanes.

The First Lady had a mischievous streak and would occasionally slip a cigarette into the fingers of a figurine. She wanted to see if the maids were being thorough. She also wondered if they ever found out who was doing it.

The President had his own "fun" with certain visitors. If someone stayed too long, Ford would quietly signal his golden retriever, "Liberty," who would rush into the office and bark, thus creating a distraction and ending the meeting.

Just before President Ford left office, he threw a surprise party for his wife. They went to a private dinner party in Georgetown. When they returned to the White House, the President suggested to Betty that they have a final dance in the darkened East Room. When the couple entered, the lights went up to reveal over a hundred friends, who joined them for a last dance.

Mrs. Ford's Cream-Cheese Roll

2 8-ounce packages of cream cheese
¼ pound butter
½ teaspoon onion juice
Pinch of salt
Ground nuts
Paprika

Cream the cheese with the butter. Add the onion juice and salt. Roll into a long roll. Roll in the ground nuts. Sprinkle with paprika. Stand in icebox. Slice thin and serve with crackers. ★

Jimmy Carter

№ 39

The Carter family came from the small town of Plains, Georgia, where they operated a large peanut farm. Before the 1976 primary election, there was not even a restaurant in town. There was The Peanut Museum, a novelty store called The Peanut Patch and a few other stores.

During his campaign, Carter held a Million Dollar Supper at "Pond House," the home of his mother, Miss Lillian. More than 400 people attended at a cost of $5,000 per ticket. Over 100 volunteers—who were referred to as The Peanut Brigade—cooked the food. Each worker wore a peanut as a name tag. Tables were fashioned from planks laid across sawhorses, and iced tea was served out of large washtubs.

There was a cake decorated with a miniature White House and a bridegroom—to represent Jimmy's honeymoon with the country. The press was not invited because Miss Lillian felt that for $5,000, a person should enjoy dinner in peace.

The influence of his family's peanut farm was seen throughout Carter's life. For example, Air Force One was referred to as "Peanut One."

The President was athletic, and when he was in Plains, he sometimes held softball games with "flacks" versus "hacks" (White House staff versus the press).

Mrs. Carter's Plains Special Cheese Ring

2 cups grated cheddar cheese
1 cup chopped walnuts
1 cup mayonnaise
1 small onion, grated
Black pepper to taste
Dash of cayenne pepper
Strawberry preserves (optional)

Combine all ingredients except preserves. Mix well and place in a 5- or 6-cup lightly greased ring mold. Refrigerate until firm for several hours or overnight. Unmold and serve plain with crackers, or fill the center with strawberry preserves. ★

"There was a lot of criticism, but I had long ago decided, do what you think is best."

—*Rosalynn Carter*

Carter Family's Eggplant Casserole

1 to 2 eggplants (about 4 pounds)
1 large mild onion, peeled and chopped
4 tablespoons butter
1½ cups crumbled corn bread
1 can (2 ounces) chopped pimientos, well drained
3 eggs, beaten
¾ teaspoon salt
¼ teaspoon pepper

Preheat oven to 350° F. Peel and chop eggplant; cook in just enough boiling salted water to cover until very soft. Drain; place in a bowl and mash until smooth. Sauté onion in butter until soft and add to eggplant. Add remaining ingredients and blend well. Pour into a well-buttered casserole dish and bake in preheated oven until firm, about 30 minutes. Serves 6–8.

Recipe courtesy of the Jimmy Carter Presidential Library. *

Rosalynn Carter enjoyed cooking and serving regional dishes. The family preferred simple foods such as homegrown vegetables and chicken casseroles. While in the White House, they frequently asked the staff to make two of their favorite recipes—cheese grits and peanut pie.

☆ The Carters were thrifty and often bought the cheapest brands of food. They made sure that leftover food was used wisely. When Henry Kissinger visited them in Plains, he was served iced tea in a Tweety Bird jelly glass.

Carter took the presidency very seriously. He was highly disciplined, and during the 1976 campaign a staff member said, "He outworked everyone."

"To go into those historic halls was an overwhelming experience for me. I was immersed in a sense of history and responsibility," said Carter. He was extremely religious, and after leaving office, he resumed teaching Sunday school and took his turn mowing the church lawn.

Amy Carter's
Peanut Butter Cookies

(President Carter's Daughter)

1 stick (½ cup) soft butter
½ cup vegetable shortening
½ cup peanut butter
1 cup granulated sugar
1 cup light brown sugar
¼ teaspoon salt
2 eggs
1 teaspoon baking soda
¼ cup warm water
3 cups sifted flour

1. Preheat oven to 400° F.
2. In a large mixing bowl, cream together butter, shortening and peanut butter.
3. Beat in the granulated and light brown sugars and salt.
4. Beat in eggs, one at a time.
5. In a small bowl, dissolve baking soda in warm water. Add to the large mixing bowl and stir well.
6. Stir in flour. Mix until dough is smooth.
7. Transfer dough to the center of a large sheet of plastic wrap; top with another sheet of equal size. Press dough out by hand to form a square 2 inches thick.
8. Wrap up tightly and refrigerate for 1 hour, or until dough is firm enough to be workable.
9. Roll dough by hand into 1-inch balls. Arrange on ungreased cookie sheets, leaving 1 to 2 inches between cookies.
10. Gently press each ball flat with the tines of a fork; press each cookie again, crosswise, to flatten to ¼-inch thickness and to create the characteristic crisscross pattern. To prevent fork from sticking, occasionally dip in flour.
11. Bake in preheated oven for 15 minutes or until golden brown.
12. Let stand for 10 minutes before transferring to wire racks to cool completely. Store in a tightly covered container.

Makes 5 dozen cookies. ★

Miss Lillian's Fried Peanuts

(President Carter's Mother)

Fill deep-fat fryer with peanut oil. Let heat to 375° F. Place blanched shelled peanuts in basket and drop down into hot oil. When white peanuts start turning brown (approximately 4–5 minutes), remove the basket. Pour peanuts out on paper towels to drain. Salt lightly while still hot. After they are cooled, place in airtight containers to keep fresh. ★

When Jimmy told his mother he was going to run for President, she inquired, "President of what?"

During his campaign, Miss Lillian came into the kitchen to find her son peeling a large number of peaches. She asked why he was doing that, and he replied, "Mother, somebody's got to peel them. If they don't get peeled and put in the freezer, they'll spoil."

Amy Carter adored her grandmother and spent a great deal of time at her house. Amy was 9 years old when her father was elected President. She was a quiet and serious child, with three older brothers, Jack, Chip and Jeff. She sometimes roller-skated in the White House, and a tree house was built for her on the South Lawn.

☆ Carter Family's Peanut Brittle

3 cups granulated sugar
1½ cups water
1 cup white corn syrup
3 cups raw peanuts
2 tablespoons (baking) soda
½ stick butter
1 teaspoon vanilla

Boil sugar, water and syrup until spins thread; add peanuts. After adding peanuts, stir continually until syrup turns golden brown. Remove from heat; add remaining ingredients; stir until butter melts. Pour quickly onto two cookie sheets with sides. As mixture begins to harden around edges, pull until thin.

Recipe courtesy of the Jimmy Carter Presidential Library. ★

The family brought a down-home feeling to the White House. For the inaugural ball, Mrs. Carter wore "an old blue dress" that she had made six years before. And at the ball, there was square dancing along with traditional dances.

The Carters wanted to share the White House with as many people as possible, and they held hundreds of formal events.

Ronald Reagan

№ 40

President Reagan's Trail Mix

1 cup salted peanuts
1 cup almonds
1 cup Brazil nuts
1 cup raisins
1 cup chocolate chips
1 cup dried date chunks
1 cup sunflower seeds
1 cup coconut chunks
1 cup pepita seeds (pumpkin seeds)

Mix listed ingredients and store in an airtight container. *

Elegance and formality returned to the White House when Ronald Reagan was elected. A glamorous style was added to parties with guests such as Frank Sinatra, Audrey Hepburn and Charlton Heston.

The First Couple knew the value of rehearsal, and photo opportunities were carefully staged. The President once told Attorney General Ed Meese, "I don't know how I could do this job if I were not an actor."

Mrs. Reagan's Sweet Potato Soufflé

1½ pounds sweet potatoes
½ cup heavy cream
3 egg yolks
⅛ teaspoon nutmeg
2 teaspoons brown sugar
4 egg whites, stiffly beaten

Preheat oven to 400° F. Prick potatoes with fork and place in buttered baking dish. Put in oven and bake 45 minutes to 1 hour. Remove from oven. Slice potatoes in half and scoop flesh into bowl. Using wire whisk or electric mixer, whip until smooth. Transfer 1¾ cups to a separate bowl. Reserve remaining potatoes for another use. Lower oven to 350° F. Blend potatoes and cream. Add egg yolks, nutmeg and brown sugar. Mix well. Fold in egg whites. Transfer mixture to a buttered 1-quart soufflé baking dish. Bake for 35–40 minutes or until a knife comes out clean. *

Mrs. Reagan's Monkey Bread ☆

1 cup milk
1 package yeast
3 eggs
3 tablespoons sugar
1 teaspoon salt
3¾ cups flour
¾ cup butter
½ cup melted butter
Two 9-inch ring molds

Scald milk in small pan. Dissolve yeast in ¼ cup milk. Cool mixture, then beat in 2 eggs. Mix dry ingredients and cut in unmelted butter. Slowly add milk mixture and blend well. Knead dough until smooth and let it rise 1 to 1½ hours. Knead it again and let it rise another 40 minutes.

Roll dough into a log shape and cut into 28 equal-size pieces. Roll each piece into a ball and coat with melted butter. Put 7 balls into the bottom of each buttered mold. Leave space between each ball. Put remaining balls on top. Let dough rise in mold for 40 minutes. Beat remaining egg and brush over the tops. Bake at 375° F for 15–20 minutes or until golden brown. ★

This bread was a Christmas favorite with the Reagans. "When you make it, you have to monkey around with it," said Mrs. Reagan.

Another "monkey connection" was the fact that Reagan co-starred with a chimpanzee in *Bedtime for Bonzo,* one of 53 movies he made. When the President was shown a photo of himself and the chimp, he responded, "I'm the one wearing the watch."

Nancy was also a successful movie star when she met Ronald. She gave up her career when they married.

Reagan was a good athlete and an excellent horseman. He initiated a therapeutic riding program for handicapped children at Rock Creek Horse Center in Washington, D.C. The children are given the experience not only of staying on a horse, but they get great satisfaction from learning to control it.

The President was fond of the White House squirrels and often brought back bags of acorns from Camp David. He'd scatter the acorns across the lawn, then enjoy watching the squirrels scurry after the nuts. When the supply ran out, Reagan said that the animals practically climbed up to his window with mournful looks.

Mrs. Reagan's Sacramento Chicken Pie

Filling
1 5- to 6-pound roaster chicken
1 green pepper
1 medium-size yellow onion, peeled
2 stalks celery
12 small white boiling onions
8 tablespoons butter
8 tablespoons flour
1 cup heavy cream
Salt and pepper to taste
Poultry seasoning to taste
2 tablespoons finely chopped fresh chives
Pie Crust
2 cups flour
1 teaspoon salt
12 tablespoons Crisco
5 to 6 tablespoons ice water

Place the chicken, green pepper, onion and celery in a large pot. Cover with water and boil for 1 hour. Remove chicken from stock; skin, bone and cut meat into small chunks. Set aside. Strain 2 cups of stock and reserve. Cover the 12 onions with water and boil for 20 minutes. Drain and set aside.

In a separate pan, melt butter, stir in the flour until it forms a smooth paste. While stirring, gradually add warm reserved stock. Cook over low heat, stirring, until mixture begins to thicken, then gradually add heavy cream, which has been warmed slightly. Season with salt, pepper and poultry seasoning. Add chives, chicken and white onions. If filling is too thick, thin with more stock.

Preheat oven to 400° F. Make pie crust by sifting the flour with the salt and mixing it with the Crisco and ice water. Roll pie dough as you would for regular pie crust.

Cut dough into two circles to fit a 3-quart casserole. Line the bottom with one circle, add filling and cover with other circle of dough. Brush the top with 2 tablespoons melted butter. Bake for 10 minutes, then reduce the heat to 350° F and bake for 30 more minutes until top crust is golden. Serves 5–6. ★

Although Nancy claimed she was not a great cook, her recipes are delicious. She modestly declared, "We all have our talents, but cooking isn't one of mine."

Chocolate was one of Reagan's favorite foods. He knew a good deal about California wines, and the White House rarely served anything else.

The Reagans entertained an average of 75,561 people per year. Over the duration of this administration, the guests included seven kings, three queens, 13 princes and 77 prime ministers. When not entertaining, the Reagans ate dinner on trays while watching the news.

Mrs. Reagan's
Stuffed Lemon Dessert

Lemons
Lemon sherbet
Mint sprigs

Cut off bottom of lemon so it will stand firmly, then slice about ½ inch off the top and save this cap. Scoop out lemon and save the juice for daiquiris to serve before luncheon. Fill the lemon shells with the best lemon sherbet you can find. Place cap of lemon back on top, plus a sprig of mint. *

The Reagans were devoted to each other and felt at home in the White House. The First Lady commented, "Ronnie still likes to say that we lived above the store."

Nancy was involved in all aspects of events. Sometimes she had a dress rehearsal to make sure everything went smoothly. The First Lady was very particular about the food served for State Dinners. The chef sometimes prepared "tryout menus" and would have Polaroid pictures taken to show how the food should be presented.

Before a dinner for Prince Charles, Chef Haller made the dessert five times before he felt it was right. Pastry chef Roland Mesnier remarked, "... the White House became a showcase of grand cuisine. She (Mrs. Reagan) was determined to have new desserts for every dinner, and she was very demanding."

One of Mrs. Reagan's first projects was to renovate the mansion's second and third floors. Some of the draperies and rugs were 20 years old, and several bathrooms dated from 1850. She worked with Ted Grabner, a decorator from Los Angeles.

Congress allotted $50,000 for this project, but the estimate for the renovations was closer to a million. Mrs. Reagan returned the money to Congress, and private donations were used instead. Twenty-one rooms were repainted, 18 carpets were replaced and new curtains made for 26 windows. Mrs. Reagan retrieved many items from the White House storerooms, and 150 pieces of furniture were renovated.

There was not enough undamaged china for a State Dinner, so new china was designed by Lenox. The 4,372-piece set was produced at a cost of $209,508.

After taking the oath of office, Reagan and his family were waiting to enter the first of several inaugural balls. "Dad is looking in the mirror, straightening his white tie, and then he cocks his head and gets that little twinkle in his eye," remembers his son Michael.

"Then he turns around, jumps straight up in the air, clicks his heels together and says, 'I'm the President of the United States of America!'"

At age 70, Reagan was the oldest President. He was able to joke about his age, describing middle age as "... when you're faced with two temptations and you choose the one that will get you home by 9 o'clock."

He also quoted Thomas Jefferson's advice about not worrying about your age. Reagan then added, "And ever since he told me that, I stopped worrying."

"What I'd really like to do is go down in history as the President who made Americans believe in themselves again."

—*Ronald Reagan*

☆ Mrs. Reagan's Crabmeat Casserole

1 14-ounce can artichoke hearts, drained
1 pound crabmeat
½ pound mushrooms
4 tablespoons butter
2½ tablespoons flour
1 cup cream
½ teaspoon salt
1 teaspoon Worcestershire sauce
¼ cup medium-dry sherry
Paprika to taste
Cayenne pepper to taste
Pepper to taste
¼ cup grated Parmesan cheese

Place artichokes in a medium-size casserole dish. Spread a layer of crabmeat over artichokes. Sauté the mushrooms and layer over crab. Melt butter in a saucepan and add remaining ingredients except cheese, stirring well after each addition to form a smooth sauce. Pour sauce over artichoke-crab layers and sprinkle cheese on top. Bake 20 minutes at 375° F. Serves 8. ★

When French President Francois Mitterand and his wife visited the White House, the Reagans hosted a State Dinner in their honor. The two couples stood in a receiving line to greet guests. When it was time for dinner, President Mitterand offered his arm to Mrs. Reagan and escorted her into the State Dining Room. President Reagan offered his arm to Mrs. Mitterand, but as they took a step forward, Mrs. Mitterand froze.

A waiter gestured toward the tables, but still Mrs. Mitterand would not move. President Reagan leaned over and whispered to her that they should proceed. Mrs. Mitterand whispered something in French, which the President couldn't understand. Finally, an interpreter ran up and said to the President, "She's telling you that you're standing on her gown!" Reagan moved his foot off her dress, and the two went into dinner.

NAVY BEANS STRING BEANS JELLIES

Reagan began the habit of eating jelly beans when he tried to stop smoking. The number of jelly beans consumed by those attending his first inauguration was reported to be 2.3 million. At Cabinet meetings, jelly beans became known as the "First Candy."

"You can tell a lot about a fellow's character by his way of eating jelly beans," the President said.

The President enjoyed the challenges of the job. He remarked, "Now I'm doing something that makes everything else I've done seem dull as dishwater when I look back."

"For eight years I was sleeping with the President, and if that doesn't give you special access, I don't know what does!"

—*Nancy Reagan*

George H.W. Bush

№ 41

Not since Martin Van Buren was elected President in 1837 had a sitting Vice President succeeded his boss to the White House (through election). George Bush responded to the news of his election by saying, "I couldn't help but think that old Martin Van Buren was up there giving me the high five sign."

Bush raced from one activity to another—consequently his Secret Service code name was "the Mexican Jumping Bean." He even raced through his golf game, and once finished 18 holes in an hour and 18 minutes.

When he was a young man, his manic pace resulted in a bleeding ulcer. As President, he measured his stress level using "the Milton Pitts test." Mr. Pitts was the White House barber who also assessed how much hair the President had lost.

George and Barbara met as teenagers at a country club dance. "I married the first man I ever kissed," said Barbara, whose maiden name is Pierce. She is a distant relative of Franklin Pierce, 14th President of the United States.

President Bush's Favorite Lemon Chicken

6 boneless chicken breasts
1 lemon, halved
Salt and pepper
Flour
Butter (2 to 3 tablespoons)
2 tablespoons vermouth
1 cup heavy cream
2 tablespoons lemon juice
Grated rind of 1 lemon
Parmesan cheese

Rub chicken breasts with lemon, salt, pepper and a little flour. Sauté in butter 7 minutes on each side. Remove from heat and arrange in baking dish. Add vermouth, cream, lemon juice and grated lemon to sauté pan. Heat thoroughly, scraping the pan to deglaze it. Strain sauce and pour over chicken breasts. Sprinkle Parmesan cheese over top and brown lightly under broiler a few minutes. Serves 6. *

Mrs. Bush's Mexican Mound

1 24-ounce bag corn chips
2 pounds ground meat
2 1¼-ounce packages taco seasoning mix
1 cup grated sharp cheese
1 small onion, chopped
10 black olives, chopped
1 tomato, chopped
1 cup sour cream
1 cup shredded lettuce
1 medium can frozen avocado dip

Place corn chips in a large wooden bowl. Prepare meat according to directions on taco seasoning mix. Place all remaining ingredients in separate bowls and put on table. Put meat in a separate bowl and place near other bowls. Allow guests to help themselves. Start by putting a layer of chips on a plate. Put on a layer of meat. Add remaining ingredients in whatever order you wish. Serves 8–10. ★

Recipe sent from the office of Mrs. Bush. She said it's a great family favorite and fun for children or guests to help with the chopping and grating.

As a young woman, Barbara found it difficult to speak in public. She gained confidence, and by the time she was First Lady, she could easily give speeches and make public appearances. She enjoyed her new role and said, "I can hardly wait to get up every morning."

As First Lady, she was involved with several educational programs, including one for literacy. Other interests included promoting volunteerism, and fighting AIDS and homelessness.

Her wit and unpretentious manner won over many critics. She was scheduled to give the commencement speech at Wellesley College, but some students objected to her image as a homemaker. She had dropped out of Smith College to get married, and the feminists thought their speaker should be a successful career woman.

Mrs. Bush defended her choices and offered this advice, "At the end of your life, you will never regret not having passed one more test, not winning one more verdict or not closing one more deal. You will regret time not spent with a husband, a child, a friend or a parent …

"Who knows? Somewhere out in this audience may even be someone who will one day follow in my footsteps and preside over the White House as the President's spouse. And I wish him well."

Mrs. Bush's Beef Cooked with Peel of Mandarin Orange

1⅓ pounds beef tenderloin slices, ⅛ inch thick
½ cup Chinese rice wine
½ ounce soy sauce
6 ounces corn oil
12 ounces chicken broth
4 dried aniseed buds
4 scallions, chopped
½ ounce fresh ginger, minced
Peel of 3 Mandarin oranges, thinly sliced
4 shakes powdered cloves
¼ pound sugar (⅔ cup plus 1 tablespoon)
¼ cup vinegar
5 dried hot red peppers
1 tablespoon salt
½ tablespoon spice powder (allspice)

Coat beef with rice wine and soy sauce. Cook in hot oil in a heavy frying pan until all liquid evaporates from beef. Add chicken broth, aniseed buds, half of the scallions, half of the ginger, orange peel, powdered cloves, sugar, vinegar and red peppers. Cover and simmer ½ hour.

Just before serving, add salt, spice powder, and remaining scallions and ginger. Red peppers may be removed. Serve hot or cold. May be frozen. Serves 4–6. ✱

The Bush grandchildren often visited the White House. A bin of toys was kept in the Oval Office, and stuffed animals inhabited the upstairs family room.

For the first family dinner at the White House, two grandchildren were missing from the table. They were discovered in the bowling alley and had requested hamburgers to be brought down. They were ordered back to the table and told not to place special orders. Family time was always a priority.

Family gatherings were often held at Walker's Point, the Bushes' vacation home in Kennebunkport, Maine. The grandchildren, who referred to President and Mrs. Bush as "Gampy" and "Ganny," called their visits "boot camp" because Ganny was so strict about making everyone pick up after themselves.

The President loved to go fishing in the coastal waters, and fresh bluefish was often served for dinner.

Ariel De Guzman, the family cook for years, said the Bushes are "very down-to-earth people who like to eat soup, salad and Chinese food. Sometimes they even have cereal for dinner."

"I thought I'd like it, but I never dreamed I would love it."

—*Barbara Bush*

Mrs. Bush's Yummy Green Beans

1 pound young green beans
4 quarts boiling water
2 tablespoons salt
2 tablespoons butter
1 clove garlic, crushed
Salt and pepper to taste

String the beans, wash well and boil rapidly in salted water, uncovered, until barely tender and still firm (taste them to make sure). Drain and run under cold water to stop the cooking. Pat dry. Melt butter and add garlic. Cook gently until softened. **Do not brown!** Pour over beans and taste for seasoning. May be made ahead. To reheat, put in microwave for 2 minutes on high heat or heat in saucepan over low heat. Serves 4. ★

Mrs. Bush claims she is not a great cook. She told this story about an egg salad disaster: "So I put on 12 hard-boiled eggs. I walked upstairs and, of course, totally forgot them. And the (Secret Service) agents came about 2½ hours later and said, 'Mrs. Bush, is there a fire going?'

"The shells were all over. The ceiling had yellow all over. The pan was gone, of course."

The President stood on the countertop to scrub and scrape the egg stains from the ceiling.

When she did cook, Barbara prepared healthy foods for her family, including lots of fish, salads and a variety of vegetables. But she didn't serve broccoli, which should come as no surprise.

Her husband made well known his dislike of that particular vegetable. His antipathy was such that he banned it from all White House menus. He once said, "I haven't liked broccoli since I was a little kid and my mother made me eat it ... I'm President of the United States, and I'm not going to eat any more broccoli."

Mrs. Bush's Vegetable Salad

2 pounds freshly chopped spinach (you chop it!)
10 hard-boiled eggs
1 pound bacon, cooked and crumbled
1 medium head of lettuce, shredded
1 cup sliced shallots
1 package frozen peas, thawed

Place in order in layers in a large salad bowl.

2½ cups mayonnaise
2½ cups sour cream
Salt and pepper
Worcestershire sauce to taste
Lemon juice to taste

Blend together and pour over peas. Add ½ cup grated Swiss cheese on top. Cover and chill for 12 hours. Do not toss. Serve. *

The family pet was a springer spaniel named "Millie." Mrs. Bush doted on the dog, and the President commented, "That dog literally comes between us at night. She wedges right up between our heads, and Bar (Barbara) likes it. She's failing with the discipline. She was better with the kids."

When Millie was pregnant, the White House staff constructed a large birthing bed in the little beauty parlor on the second floor. As the time for the birth drew near, Mrs. Bush moved her desk into the parlor so she could keep watch over the dog. The First Lady assisted the veterinarian as Millie gave birth. One puppy named "Spotty" lived at the White House with President George W. Bush.

The First Lady published *Millie's Book,* "as dictated to Barbara Bush." Millie made $889,176 in royalties, which Mrs. Bush donated to charity.

Later the President quipped, "Study hard, and you might grow up to be President. But let's face it; even then, you'll never make as much money as your dog."

Doro's Tex-Mex Dip

Recipe from Dorothy Bush Koch (President Bush's Daughter)

7 scallions, chopped
2 medium tomatoes, diced
1½ cups shredded lettuce
1 cup shredded sharp cheddar cheese
1 10½-ounce can ripe pitted olives, drained and chopped
1 cup chunky picante sauce (mild or hot)
1 12½-ounce can chili (no beans)
1 cup guacamole or 2 ripe avocados, seeded, peeled and diced
1 14½-ounce can refried beans
1 cup sour cream
Cilantro sprigs, stems removed
Lemon or lime wedges (optional)
Corn chips or tortilla chips for serving

In a large bowl, combine three-quarters of the scallions, tomatoes, lettuce, cheese and olives. Add picante sauce, chili, guacamole, refried beans and sour cream. Blend mixture gently.

Transfer dip to one large or two smaller serving bowls. Level top. Garnish with remaining scallions, tomatoes, lettuce, cheese and olives in colorful rows arranged on top of the dip.

 Garnish edges with sprigs of cilantro and lime or lemon wedges to squeeze over dip, if desired. Surround dip with baskets or smaller containers filled with your favorite store-bought corn chips or tortilla chips. Serves 24.

Reprinted with the permission of Scribner, an imprint of Simon & Schuster Adult Publishing Group, from *The Bush Family Cookbook* by Ariel De Guzman. © 2005 by Ariel De Guzman. ✳

In 1992, Doro Bush became the first bride to be married at Camp David. The President thought the wedding was to be informal and had to borrow a tie from the groom. He walked his daughter down the aisle wearing an old pair of white pants.

As a prank, the groom's brother put Bush reelection stickers on the bottom of the groom's shoes.

After her husband retired from the presidency, Mrs. Bush had this to say about their home life: "George is the best little dishwasher in Texas." George disagreed and said, "Barbara makes the bed. I make the coffee. And Millie (the dog) does the dishes."

"I really love the job."

—*George H.W. Bush*

William J. Clinton

№ 42

Elvis' Sandwich

A Favorite of President Clinton

2 slices white bread
3 tablespoons peanut butter
1 small banana
2 tablespoons butter

Toast bread lightly and spread one slice with peanut butter. Place banana on the other slice, then sandwich the two pieces together. Melt butter in a small skillet and grill sandwich on each side until golden brown. Cut diagonally and serve. ★

President Clinton is a big fan of Elvis Presley and has a collection of his records and memorabilia.

When the Clintons moved into the White House, they converted a chef's kitchen off the President's Dining Room into a family kitchen. Hillary said, "Our kitchen is the place where Bill and I eat dinner together or have a glass of champagne after an event, or raid the refrigerator for leftovers when we come home late after attending a dinner at which we found no time to eat!"

This was a comfortable room, and the President sometimes sat there with the butlers to watch basketball games.

Mrs. Clinton continued the White House Endowment Fund, which had been started by Barbara Bush as a means to pay for future renovations to the Executive Mansion. The project eventually exceeded its $25 million goal.

The First Lady took a great interest in the history of the house and read 40 books on the subject. Then she wrote her own book in 2000—*An Invitation to the White House* included an insider's look at how the White House is operated.

Mrs. Clinton hired Kaki Hockersmith to redecorate the state rooms. *House Beautiful* praised the newly redone Blue Room as "an interior that shows off America at its best." The First Lady was involved during the entire process, and the President even helped pick out fabric swatches.

President Clinton's Favorite Chicken Enchiladas

1 tablespoon plus ⅓ cup oil
2 4-ounce cans chopped green chilies
1 large clove garlic, minced
1 28-ounce can tomatoes
2 cups chopped onion
2 teaspoons salt
½ teaspoon oregano
3 cups shredded cooked chicken
2 cups sour cream
2 cups grated cheddar cheese
15 corn or flour tortillas

Preheat 1 tablespoon oil in a skillet. Sauté chilies and garlic in oil. Drain and chop the tomatoes, reserving ½ cup of the juice. Add these to the pan, along with the onion, 1 teaspoon salt and oregano. Simmer, uncovered, until thick, about 30 minutes. Put mixture in a bowl and set aside.

Combine chicken with sour cream, grated cheese and 1 teaspoon salt. Heat ⅓ cup oil; dip tortillas in oil until they become limp. Drain well on paper towels. Fill tortillas with chicken mixture; roll up and arrange side by side, seam down, in a 9" x 13" baking dish. Pour tomato mixture over the top. Bake at 350° F for 20 minutes. Yields 15 enchiladas. ∗

 The Clinton White House served primarily American cuisine and wines. Mrs. Clinton forbade menus to be written in French.

The head chef, Pierre Chambrin, was told to prepare foods with a lower fat content, and the First Lady sent 30 cookbooks down to him. Chambrin resigned within a year and was replaced by Walter Scheib from the Greenbrier Resort. Scheib prepared more American-style dishes, and once served buffalo meat at a NATO dinner.

For the most part, the Clintons enjoyed living in the White House. The First Lady described what it was like to stand on the Truman Balcony at sunset: "Looking out at the Washington Monument and the Jefferson Monument across the fountain, there is a sense of magic and beauty unmatched."

The security of the First Family is the primary concern for the Secret Service. It was difficult for the President to go out spontaneously. At least 30 minutes lead time was necessary to organize a motorcade, and agents had to check out the destination beforehand.

If Clinton ate at a restaurant, the Secret Service supervised all food preparation. On one visit to Capitol Hill, the President asked for a cup of decaf coffee. An agent was dispatched to bring one back from the White House.

Mrs. Clinton's Chocolate Chip Cookies

1½ cups unsifted flour
1 teaspoon salt
1 teaspoon baking soda
1 cup solid vegetable shortening
1 cup light brown sugar
½ cup granulated sugar
1 teaspoon vanilla
2 eggs
2 cups old-fashioned rolled oats
12 ounces semisweet chocolate chips

Preheat oven to 350° F. Grease baking sheets. Combine flour, salt and baking soda. In a separate bowl, beat together shortening, sugars and vanilla until creamy. Add eggs, beating until light and fluffy. Gradually beat in flour mixture and rolled oats. Stir in chocolate chips.

Drop batter by teaspoonfuls onto baking sheets. Bake 8–10 minutes or until golden. Cool for 2 minutes. Place cookies on a wire rack to cool completely. *

These cookies beat Barbara Bush's chocolate chip cookies and Elizabeth Dole's pecan rolls in a cookie baking contest sponsored by *Family Circle* magazine.

Hillary Clinton once remarked, "I suppose I could have stayed home and baked cookies and had teas. But what I decided to do was pursue my profession."

When this comment was interpreted as a criticism of women who'd decided to stay home to raise their children, Mrs. Clinton, in a lighthearted jest, served cookies to reporters at a press conference and had thousands of her cookies distributed at the 1992 Democratic National Convention, where her husband received the nomination for President.

After Bill retired from the presidency after two terms in office, Hillary Clinton remained active in politics and was later elected senator from the state of New York.

Arkansas Fried Pie

Pie Dough
3½ cups flour
2 teaspoons baking powder
Pinch of salt
1 cup shortening
1 cup cheddar cheese
1 12-ounce can evaporated milk

Pie Filling
6 ripe pears or apples
4 tablespoons brown sugar
2 tablespoons water
1 tablespoon flour
1 teaspoon cinnamon

Combine first five ingredients in bowl. Slowly add evaporated milk, and knead dough until smooth. Cover bowl and put in refrigerator for 1 hour. Peel and core fruit, and cut into pieces. Place in a pan with remaining ingredients. Cover and cook over low heat until fruit is soft. Remove from heat and mash fruit.

When dough is chilled, place on a flat surface that has been lightly dusted with flour. Roll out dough to about ⅛ inch thick. Cut into 5-inch squares. Put fruit filling in middle of square, and fold opposite corners together to make a triangle. Crimp edges together with a fork.

 Put 1½ cups of oil in a heavy iron skillet. Put pan on stove and set burner to medium-high. When oil is hot, place several pies in oil, and fry until golden brown on one side. Flip and cook other side. Remove from pan and place on paper towels to drain. Repeat until all pies are cooked. Combine 1 tablespoon sugar with 1 teaspoon cinnamon; sprinkle over top of pies. *

President Clinton was proud of being from Arkansas. He liked to show people around his home state and have them sample a fried pie, an Arkansas specialty. He was a talented musician and played his saxophone at several inaugural balls.

The Clintons' teenage daughter, Chelsea, turned the White House solarium into a hangout area for her friends. They had "Bunking Parties" and munched on pizza in the State Dining Room. She was an avid soccer player and ballet enthusiast, and her favorite subjects in school were math and foreign languages.

As part of the celebrations marking the bicentennial of the White House, the Clintons had the Lenox Company design 300 new place settings of china. The plates are bordered in pale yellow, and images of the mansion replaced the presidential seal. The first time the china was used was for a dinner attended by former Presidents Ford, Carter and Bush and their wives, along with Lady Bird Johnson.

President Clinton's favorite food was the type served at McDonald's or Dunkin' Donuts. One source said, "Clinton's idea of a good meal is a Happy Meal." He can't eat chocolate or dairy products. His favorite desserts are pear soufflé, strawberry cake, and cherry or apple pie.

In order to control his weight, Clinton went jogging three to five times a week. He didn't like the track at the White House, so he was driven to a park along the Potomac River. The 10-car motorcade needed to transport the President included the President's limousine, motorcycle police, police cars, the Secret Service SWAT team, an ambulance, a press van, a communications truck, and a van to pick up any team members who couldn't keep up with Clinton.

"Being President is like running a cemetery: you've got a lot of people under you and nobody's listening."

—*Bill Clinton*

☆ Arkansas Fried Green Tomatoes

3 medium-size green tomatoes
½ cup flour
½ teaspoon salt
½ teaspoon garlic powder
⅛ teaspoon cayenne pepper
¼ teaspoon black pepper
2 eggs
1 tablespoon water
¾ cup yellow cornmeal
1 to 1½ cups oil for frying

Cut tomatoes into thin slices. Have ready three shallow bowls. In first bowl, mix flour, salt, garlic powder and both types of pepper. In second bowl, beat eggs with water. Put cornmeal in third bowl. Dredge tomato slice in flour mixture, then in egg and finally in cornmeal. Set aside and repeat until all tomatoes are used.

Put oil in skillet and heat to 350° F. When oil is hot, put in enough tomato slices to cover bottom of pan. Cook until brown on one side. Flip and brown the other side. Place on paper towels to drain, and cook remaining tomatoes. ★

As the year 2000 approached, the Clintons decided to host a series of Millennium Evenings to "highlight the creativity and inventiveness of the American people."

Some of the featured participants were Poet Laureate Robert Pinsky, former Poet Laureates Robert Hass and Rita Dove, Pulitzer Prize-winning historian Bernard Bailyn and Professor Stephen Hawking. Elie Wiesel spoke on "The Perils of Indifference" and said, "If we don't have hope, we must invent it."

The Millennium Evening on September 16, 1998, featured a jazz performance by Wynton Marsalis and Marian McPartland. In the audience was President Václav Havel of the Czech Republic. Mrs. Clinton later wrote, "His presence, as a leader in the fight for democracy in his own country, made the experience even more meaningful." Other guests of honor were Henry Kissinger and Kurt Vonnegut.

"It was, for me, an isolating and lonely experience."
—Hillary Clinton

☆ Menu for the Dinner in Honor of His Excellency Václav Havel President of the Czech Republic And Mrs. Havlová

Gingered Pheasant Consommé
Ravioli of Chanterelles and Sweet Potatoes
Pheasant Confit on Lemon Spinach

Roasted Salmon with Honey Spice Glaze
Carrot and Corn Risotto
Charred Tomato Compote

Baked Artichokes
Oregano Marinated Goat Cheese
Late Summer Greens and Chive Garlic Dressing

Caramel Rum Raisin Ice Cream
Poached Pear in Red Wine Sauce
Sour Cherry Pâté de Fruit
Hazelnut Gianduja Vanilla Pretzel

Lewis "Reserve" Chardonnay 1996
Archery Summit Pinot Noir 1994
Roederer "White House Cuvée" 1991

George W. Bush

№ 43

Geor W. is the oldest son of George H.W. Bush, the 41st President, and they jokingly refer to each other as "43" and "41." When his son was elected, the former President said he felt the "... pride of a father in a son, and it transcends or avoids the issues."

This was the second time in American history that a President's son was elected. The sixth President, John Quincy Adams, was the son of John Adams, the second President and one of the country's founding fathers.

"Celebrating America's Spirit Together" was the theme for George W.'s first inaugural celebrations. Many of the events referred to Bush's home state of Texas.

For the Black Tie and Boots Inaugural Ball, the Fort Worth Zoo supplied a menagerie of animals— an armadillo, roadrunner, alligator, Harris hawk, screech owl and barn owl. Also in attendance was "Bevo," the University of Texas longhorn mascot.

The new President reluctantly took to the dance floor with his wife. He apologized for his poor dancing skills, saying, "I confess I'm not the world's greatest dancer, but you're going to have to suffer through it."

Mrs. Bush's Smoked Shrimp with Mango Salsa

2 very ripe mangoes, diced
1 cucumber, peeled, seeded and diced
½ red bell pepper, finely chopped
¼ red onion, finely chopped
1 jalapeño pepper, diced
¼ cup chopped cilantro
¼ cup lime juice
1 tablespoon minced ginger
1 tablespoon brown sugar
Salt to taste
1 loaf bread
24 shrimp (21–25 size), smoked or herb grilled, split lengthwise

Combine the fruit, vegetables and seasonings. Purée ⅙ of the mixture to make a spread. Cut 48 bread rounds and oven-dry or toast. Spread puréed mixture over bread rounds. Top each with half a shrimp and some of the unpuréed mango salsa. Garnish with scallions and a cilantro leaf. Makes 48 tea sandwiches. ★

President and Laura Bush's Deviled Eggs

12 large eggs, hard-boiled and peeled
1 tablespoon soft butter
1 tablespoon mayonnaise
1 tablespoon Dijon mustard
½ teaspoon Yucatan Sunshine habanero pepper
  sauce*
Salt to taste

Cut eggs in half and set whites aside. Put egg yolks in a food processor and add all other ingredients. Process for 20 seconds or until mixture has blended. Check for taste and increase butter, mayonnaise, mustard and seasonings if desired. Place mixture in a pastry bag with star tip and pipe into egg white halves. Sprinkle with paprika and chopped parsley. Chill for about an hour before serving.

  *Yucatan Sunshine habanero sauce is preferred by the Bushes. They used it while living in Texas, and now the White House chef uses it in a variety of recipes. Yucatan Sunshine and other Luzianne pepper sauces can be found at most larger supermarkets nationwide, but Tabasco sauce can be substituted. *

☆ Mrs. Bush enjoys living in the White House. "Just the fact of living in a house that Abraham Lincoln once lived in is unbelievable. It's really, really fabulous," she said. "And the whole history of the country ... is documented by the lives of the people who live in the White House."

White House Pastry Chef Roland Mesnier had this to say about the 43rd President's wife: "First Lady Laura Bush is meticulous—and the house is sparkling. She has a great knowledge of food and how it should be prepared ..."

In February of 2005, Mrs. Bush promoted Cristeta Comerford to the position of Executive Chef. A member of the kitchen staff for 10 years, Ms. Comerford is of Asian descent, and is the first minority and the first woman to become head chef of the White House. Her job includes balancing the demands of official entertaining with the meals for Bush family dinners.

Ms. Comerford prefers to use fresh foods when available. The White House kitchen is a modest, no-frills commercial kitchen with 12 burners and five sinks.

"Do I aspire to be up there at the top of the list? Absolutely. While you have this forum, you want to be as constructive for your country as you possibly can."

—Laura Bush

Shortly before he became President, Bush bought a 1,583-acre ranch in Crawford, Texas. Laura teased her husband about his initial lack of farming skills.

"George didn't know much about ranches when we bought the place. Andover and Yale don't have a real strong ranching program," she said. "But I'm proud of George. He's learned a lot about ranching since that first year when he tried to milk the horse."

The President likes the informal atmosphere at the ranch and enjoys clearing brush from the property. Cutting invasive trees and hauling off the debris is hard, dusty work. Bush frequently lassos his Cabinet members into action, but so far Secretary of State Condoleezza Rice has escaped "brush duty." The manual labor is therapeutic for Bush. His deputy chief of staff, Joseph Hagin, says it's hard to discuss politics over the sound of chain saws.

"We like to go for rides at our ranch, before dinner," says Mrs. Bush. "He's a windshield cowboy, as he says, which means he drives a pickup. We drive down into the bottoms of the creekbeds and riverbeds. And we do that nearly every time we're there, nearly every day ... it's really the only time we're alone like that, in a car. That's fun!"

Several heads of state have been guests at the ranch. The President is comfortable in jeans and cowboy boots, and when important guests arrive, he drives his pickup to the heliport to greet them.

In 2001, Russian President Vladimir Putin and his wife visited. They were treated to a chuckwagon supper featuring mesquite-smoked beef tenderloin, southern-fried catfish and Blue Bell vanilla ice cream (a local favorite). After dinner, the couple was taught a regional dance called the "cotton-eyed Joe."

Mrs. Bush's Cowboy Cookies

3 cups flour
1 tablespoon baking powder
1 tablespoon baking soda
1 tablespoon cinnamon
1 teaspoon salt
1½ cups butter
1½ cups sugar
1½ cups light brown sugar
3 eggs
1 tablespoon vanilla
3 cups semisweet chocolate chips
3 cups old-fashioned rolled oats
2 cups flaked coconut
2 cups chopped pecans

Preheat oven to 350° F. Mix flour, baking powder, baking soda, cinnamon and salt in a bowl. In an 8-quart bowl, beat butter on medium speed until smooth and creamy, about 1 minute. Gradually beat in sugars; beat to combine, about 2 minutes. Add eggs, one at a time, beating after each. Beat in vanilla. Stir in flour mixture until just combined. Add chocolate chips, oats, coconut and pecans.

For each cookie, drop ¼ cup dough onto ungreased baking sheets, spacing 3 inches apart. Bake at 350° F for 10–12 minutes or until edges are lightly browned; rotate sheets halfway through.

 Remove cookies onto wire racks to cool. Yields about 3 dozen cookies.

To make 6 dozen small cookies, use 2 tablespoons dough for each. Bake for 8–10 minutes. ★

Mrs. Bush's Guacamole

8 avocados
7 shallots, chopped fine
4 lemons, juiced
1 tablespoon salt
1 teaspoon black pepper
1 jalapeño pepper, seeded and chopped
½ bunch cilantro

Blend all ingredients with a hand mixer. ★

"People would be surprised how real life in the White House is, and how normal. I mean, it's magnificent, and we live with furniture and art that's literally museum quality, with a wonderful staff and a chef and all those things that are true luxuries. We have friends over for holiday parties—nearly every bedroom is filled with friends."

—*Laura Bush*

Mrs. Bush's Vegetable Soup

1¼ cups pinto beans, soaked overnight and
    drained
1 teaspoon salt
1 bay leaf
1 teaspoon dried oregano
1 pound tomatoes, fresh or canned, peeled,
    seeded and chopped; juice reserved
2 ancho chilies
1 pound mixed summer squash
4 ears of corn (about 2 cups kernels)
2 tablespoons corn or vegetable oil
2 yellow onions, cut into ¼-inch squares
2 cloves garlic, finely chopped
2 tablespoons red chili powder, or more to taste
1 teaspoon ground cumin
½ teaspoon ground coriander
8 ounces green beans, cut into 1-inch lengths
4 ounces Jack or Muenster cheese, grated
½ bunch cilantro, roughly chopped
Whole cilantro leaves for garnish

Cook the presoaked beans for about 1–2 hours in
plenty of water with the salt, bay leaf and oregano.
Remove them from the heat when they are soft but
not mushy, as they will continue to cook in the
stew. Drain the beans and save the broth. Prepare
the tomatoes. Open the chili pods and remove the
seeds and veins; then cut the chilies into narrow

strips. Cut the squash into large pieces. Shave the
kernels from the corn.

Heat the oil in a large skillet, and sauté the onions
over high heat for 1–2 minutes. Lower the heat;
add the garlic, chili powder, cumin and coriander
and stir everything together. Add a little bean broth.
Stir in the squash, corn, green beans, and chili
strips along with the cooked beans and enough
broth to make a fairly wet stew. Cook slowly until
the vegetables are done, about 15–20 minutes.

Taste the stew and adjust the seasoning. Stir in
the cheese and chopped cilantro, and garnish with
whole leaves of cilantro. Serve with corn bread or
tortillas. A great one-dish meal if you have a
garden or have just visited the farmers market. ★

At the 2005 White House Correspondent's
dinner, Mrs. Bush stole the spotlight from her
husband. He had started telling a joke when she
interrupted. To the President's surprise, she took
over the microphone and told the audience that
her husband would normally be in bed by now.

"Nine o'clock, Mr. Excitement here is sound
asleep, and I'm watching *Desperate Housewives*—
with Lynne Cheney. Ladies and gentlemen, I am
a desperate housewife. I mean, if those women
on that show think they're desperate, they oughta
be with George." She offered this advice to her
husband: "George, if you really want to end tyranny
in the world, you're going to have to stay up later."

Mrs. Bush's Hot Chocolate

6 tablespoons cocoa (unsweetened)
Pinch of salt
6 tablespoons sugar
2½ cups milk
2½ cups light cream
Pinch of cinnamon
½ teaspoon vanilla
Whipped cream, cocoa powder and orange zest

Mix cocoa, salt and sugar in a pan. Add milk. Heat to dissolve. Add cream, cinnamon and vanilla. Heat to just under boiling. Mix well and pour into warm mugs. Top with whipped cream, cocoa powder and orange zest. Serves 4. *

A cup of this hot chocolate takes the chill out of a winter evening.

Mrs. Bush claims she's not great in the kitchen (although these recipes are delicious!). "I haven't had to cook in a few years. It's been a great relief for my family," she joked.

The President likes to make pancakes with the couple's twin daughters, Barbara and Jenna. When the girls were young, George and Laura divided up the household chores. The First Lady remarked, "He always took the clothes to the laundry ... I did nearly all the cooking, although he was famous for pancakes. Pancakes à la George. Or the chopped-egg sandwich à la George."

The First Family has a cat named "Willie" and two Scottish terriers, "Barney" and "Miss Beazley." Barney will give you a dog's eye view of the White House via his "Barney Cam." Check out *whitehousekids.gov* and click on the "Videos" link.

Barney takes viewers on tours of the mansion, showing off the spring gardens as well as the Christmas decorations. There are delightful scenes of the President playing in the snow with Barney, and Ari Fleischer (former Press Secretary) is caught playing poker with the dog.

In "Where in the White House is Miss Beazley?", Barney is disappointed at not being named to the Cabinet, so the President tells him he has the important job of taking care of the new puppy. Supporting roles are played by the President's friends and advisors, including Lynne Cheney, Attorney General Alberto Gonzales, Andy Card (former Chief of Staff) and Cristeta Comerford, the head chef.

"To those of you who received honors, awards and distinctions, I say well done. And to the C students, I say you, too, can be President of the United States."

—*George W. Bush*

Presidential Nicknames

Washington	Father of His Country, Sword of the Revolution
John Adams	His Rotundity, Atlas of Independence
Jefferson	The Sage of Monticello, The Red Fox, Long Tom, Man of the People
Madison	The Father of the Constitution, Jemmy, Little Jamie
Monroe	The Last Cocked Hat (because he was the last of the Dynasty of Virginia Presidents?), The Era of Good Feelings President
John Q. Adams	The Puritan, Old Man Eloquent, King John II
Jackson	Old Hickory, King Andrew, Hero of New Orleans, The Sage of the Hermitage
Van Buren	The Little Magician, Martin Van Ruin, Little Van, The Flying Dutchman, Machiavellian Belshazzar, Red Fox of Kinderhook
W.H. Harrison	Granny Harrison, Tippecanoe, Old Tip
Tyler	His Accidency, Traitor Tyler
Polk	The Plodder, Young Hickory, Napoleon of the Stump
Taylor	Old Rough and Ready, Old Zach
Fillmore	Wool Carder President, American Louis Philippe
Pierce	The Fainting General, Young Hickory of the Granite Hills, Handsome Frank
Buchanan	Old Fogey, Old Buck, Ten-Cent Jimmy, Old Public Functionary
Lincoln	Honest Abe, The Great Emancipator, The Illinois Ape, Illinois Rail-Splitter
A. Johnson	The Drunken Tailor, Tennessee Tailor, Sir Veto, Andy Veto, Andy, Old Andy
Grant	The Hero of Appomattox, Unconditional Surrender Grant, The Old Man
Hayes	His Fraudulency, Ruther*fraud* B. Hayes, The Usurper, The Great Unknown, Old 8 to 7, Dark Horse President
Garfield	Boatman Jim, The Canal Boy, Preacher President
Arthur	Elegant Arthur, The Gentleman Boss, The Prince of Hospitality, Chet
Cleveland	Uncle Jumbo, The Buxom Buffalonian, His Obstinacy, The Veto President, Grover the Good, Hangman of Buffalo

B. Harrison	The Icebox, The White House Iceberg (his handshake "was like a wilted Petunia"), Little Ben (he was 5-foot-6), Young Tippecanoe, Kid Gloves Harrison	☆ Carter	Jimmy, Jimmy Peanut, Peanut President
McKinley	The Stocking-Footed Orator, The Idol of Ohio, The Major	Reagan	The Gipper, Dutch, Teflon President, Rawhide (his Secret Service code name), The Great Communicator
T. Roosevelt	Rough Rider, The Hero of San Juan Hill, Trust Buster, TR, Teddy (he hated that nickname)	G.H.W. Bush	Poppy, #41, Bush Sr.
Taft	Big Bill (he weighed 300 to 350 pounds), Godknows Taft, Peaceful Bill	Clinton	Slick Willie, Bubba, Big Dog
Wilson	Schoolmaster in Politics, Tommy	G.W. Bush	Dubya, Bush Jr., #43, Uncurious George, King George
Harding	President Hardly		
Coolidge	Silent Cal, Cautious Cat, Red		
Hoover	The Great Engineer, The Chief, Great Humanitarian		
F.D. Roosevelt	FDR, The Champ, That Man in the White House		
Truman	The New Missouri Compromise, Give 'em Hell Harry, High Tax Harry, Haberdasher Harry		
Eisenhower	Ike (campaign slogan was "I Like Ike")		
Kennedy	JFK, Jack, King of Camelot		
Johnson	LBJ, Landslide Lyndon		
Nixon	Tricky Dick, The Trickster		
Ford	Mr. Nice Guy, Jerry, Jerry the Jerk		

"Don't sit up nights thinking about making me President, for that will never come and I have no ambition in that direction. Any party which would nominate me would make me a great mistake."

—William H. Taft

Bibliography

Cookbooks listed in chronological order

The Art of Cookery Made Plain and Easy, Hanna Glasse. England, 1747.

The House-Keeper's Pocket-Book, and Compleat Family Cook, Sarah Harrison. Sixth edition. London: R. Ware, 1755.

American Cookery, Amelia Simmons. Hudson and Goodwin, 1796.

The Virginia Housewife or, Methodical Cook, Mary Randolph. Philadelphia: E.H. Butler & Co., 1860. First published in Washington, D.C., 1824.

The Cook Not Mad, or Rational Cookery; Being a Collection of Original and Selected Receipts, Author unknown. Watertown, N.Y.: Knowlton & Rice, 1831.

The Cook's Own Book: Being a Complete Culinary Encyclopedia, by a Boston Housekeeper (Mrs. N.K.M. Lee). Boston: Munroe & Francis, 1832.

The Cook's Own Book and Housekeeper's Register, Eliza Leslie. Boston, 1835.

The Good Housekeeper, or, the Way to Live Well, and to Be Well While We Live, Sarah Josepha Hale. Boston: Otis, Broaders, 1841 (first edition, 1839).

The American Frugal Housewife, Lydia Maria Child. New York: Samuel S. and William Wood, 1844.

Improved Housewife; or, Book of Receipts; with Engravings for Marketing and Carving, by a Married Lady (Mrs. A.L. Webster). Hartford, Conn.: 1847.

A Mother's Book of Traditional Household Skills, L.G. Abell. The Skillful Housewife's Books originally published by R.T. Young, 1852.

The American Home Cook Book, by an American Lady. New York: Dick and Fitzgerald, 1854.

Miss Beecher's Domestic Receipt-Book, Catharine E. Beecher. New York: Harper & Brothers, Publishers, 1858.

Book of Household Management, Mrs. Beaton (Isabella Mary). London, 1861 (first edition, 1859).

Mrs. Hill's New Cook Book, a Practical System for Private Families, in Town and Country, Mrs. A.P. Hill. New York: Carleton, Publisher, 1870.

Breakfast, Luncheon and Tea, Marion Harland. New York: Scribner, Armstrong & Co., 1875.

Buckeye Cookery and Practical Housekeeping, Compiled from Original Recipes, Author unknown. Minneapolis: Buckeye Publishing Company, 1877.

Practical Cooking and Dinner Giving, Mary F. Henderson. New York: Harper & Brothers, Publishers, 1878.

Dixie Cook Book, Estelle Woods Wilcox. L.A. Clarkson & Co., 1883.

Boston Cooking-School Cook Book, Mrs. D.A. Lincoln, 1884.

The Woman Suffrage Cook Book, Hattie A. Burr. Boston: Published by Hattie A. Burr, 1886.

The White House Cook Book, A Comprehensive Cyclopedia of Information for the Home, Hugo Ziemann & Mrs. F.L. Gillette. Chicago: The Werner Company, 1887.

Margery Daw in the Kitchen and What She Learned There, Lucy Bostwick. Auburn, N.Y.: Standard (Watson), 1887.

Statesmen's Dishes and How to Cook Them, Mrs. Benjamin Harrison. Washington, D.C.: The National Tribune, 1890.

Our Own Cook Book, Compiled by the Ladies of the First Presbyterian Church, Galena, Ill. Gazette Printing House, 1892.

The Century Cook Book, Mary Ronald. New York: The Century Co., 1895.

The 1896 Boston Cooking-School Cook Book, Fannie Merritt Farmer. New York: Gramercy Books, 1896.

The Way to a Man's Heart, "The Settlement" Cook Book, compiled by Mrs. Simon Kander. Milwaukee: J.H. Yewdale & Sons, Co., 1901.

Rumford Complete Cook Book, Lily Haxworth Wallace. Providence, R.I.: The Rumford Chemical Works, 1908.

A New Book of Cookery, Fannie Merritt Farmer, 1912.

The Economy Administration Cook Book, Susie Root Rhodes. Hammond, Ind.: W.B. Conkey Co., 1913.

The Congressional Club Cook Book, Revised Edition. Compiled and published by The Congressional Club, Washington, D.C., 1933.

The Williamsburg Art of Cookery, The Colonial Williamsburg Foundation. New York: Hold, Rinehart and Winston, 1938.

The Martha Washington Cook Book, Marie Kimball. New York: Coward-McCann, 1940.

The Congressional Club Cook Book, Third Edition. Compiled and published by The Congressional Club, Washington, D.C., 1948.

The Presidential Cookbook, Feeding the Roosevelts and Their Guests, Henrietta Nesbitt. Garden City, N.Y.: Doubleday & Company, Inc. 1951.

Who Says We Can't Cook!, Members of the Women's National Press Club. Washington, D.C: McIver Art and Publications, Inc., 1955.

A Treasury of White House Cooking, François Rysavy, as told to Frances Spatz Leighton. New York: G.P. Putnam's Sons, 1957.

The Art of Creole Cookery, William I. Kaufman and Sister Mary Ursula Cooper, O.P. Garden City, N.Y: Doubleday & Company, Inc., 1962.

The White House Cookbook, Janet Halliday Ervin. Chicago: Follett Publishing Company, 1964.

The Congressional Club Cook Book, Seventh Edition. Compiled and published by The Congressional Club, Washington, D.C., 1965.

The President's Cookbook, Poppy Cannon & Patricia Brooks. Funk & Wagnall's, 1968.

The Congressional Club Cook Book, Eighth Edition. Compiled and published by The Congressional Club, Washington, D.C., 1970.

James Beard's American Cookery, James Beard. Boston: Little, Brown and Company, 1972.

Marny Clifford's Washington Cookbook, Marny Clifford. New York: E.P. Dutton & Co. Inc., 1972.

Woodrow Wilson House Cookbook, The National Trust for Historic Preservation, Washington, D.C., 1974.

The Thirteen Colonies Cookbook, Mary Donovan, Amy Hatrak, Frances Mills, Elizabeth Shull. New York: Praeger Publishers, Inc., 1975.

Thomas Jefferson's Cook Book, Maria Kimball. Charlottesville, Va.: University Press of Virginia, 1976.

The Congressional Club Cook Book, Ninth Edition. Compiled and published by The Congressional Club, Washington, D.C., 1976.

The Good Cook's Companion, Audrey Senturia and Ruth Ann Rubin. Dublin, N.H.: Yankee, Inc., 1981.

The Joy of Cooking, Irma S. Rombauer and Marion Rombauer Becker. Indianapolis: Bobbs-Merrill Company, Inc., 1981. Also published in New York.

The First Ladies' Cook Book, Parents Magazine Enterprises. New York: GMG Publishing, 1982.

The Washington Cookbook, Volume 1, The Washington Opera. The McArdle Printing Company, Inc. 1982.

The Congressional Club Cook Book, Tenth Edition. Compiled and published by The Congressional Club, Washington, D.C., 1982.

The White House Family Cookbook, Henry Haller with Virginia Aronson. New York: Random House, Inc., 1987.

The Congressional Club Cook Book, Eleventh Edition. Compiled and published by The Congressional Club, Washington, D.C., 1987.

Monroe Family Recipes, Judith D. Kosik, editor. Ash Lawn-Highland, College of William and Mary, 1988.

Dining with the Hoover Family, Dale C. Mayer. West Branch, Iowa: Herbert Hoover Presidential Library, 1991.

Cooking in the Young Republic, Patricia B. Mitchell. Chatham, Va.: Mitchells Publications, 1992.

The Civil War Cookbook, William C. Davis. Philadelphia: Courage Books, 1993.

Early American Cookbook—Authentic Favorites by Historical Figures, Dr. Kristie Lynn and Robert W. Pelton. Boca Raton, Fla.: Cool Hand Communications, Inc., 1994.

The Washington Cookbook, Volume 2, The Washington Opera. The McArdle Printing Company, Inc., 1994.

★ White House Cook Book, Revised Edition. Hugo Ziemann. Revisions by Patti Bazel Geil, RD and Tami Ross, RD. New York: John Wiley & Sons, 1996.

Miss Lillian and Friends, Beth Tartan and Ruby Hayes. New York: A&W Publishers, 1997.

Civil War Recipes, Receipts from the Pages of Godey's Lady's Book, Lily May Spaulding and John Spaulding, editors. Lexington, Ky.: The University Press of Kentucky, 1999.

An Invitation to the White House, Hillary Rodham Clinton. New York: Simon & Schuster, 2000.

Monpelier Hospitality, The Montpelier Foundation, Virginia, 2002.

The Penguin Companion to Food, Alan Davidson. New York: Penguin Books, 2002.

The American History Cookbook, Mark H. Zanger. Westport, Conn.: Greenwood Press, 2003.

The U.S. History Cookbook, Joan D'Amico and Karen Eich Drummond. Hoboken, N.J.: John Wiley & Sons, Inc., 2003.

The Clinton Presidential Center Cookbook, Shannon Butler and Nealon DeVore, editors. Little Rock, Ark.: The William J. Clinton Presidential Foundation, 2003.

That Palace in Washington, Patricia B. Mitchell. Mitchells Publications, 2004.

Delicacies in Proportion, Patricia B. Mitchell. Mitchells Publications, 2004.

On Food and Cooking, The Science and Lore of the Kitchen, Harold McGee. New York: Scribner, 2004.

Plain Food and High Thinking, Patricia B. Mitchell. Mitchells Publications, 2005.

The Bush Family Cookbook, Ariel De Guzman. New York: Simon & Schuster, 2005.

Non-Cookbook Sources

Perley's Reminiscences, Ben: Perley Poore. Philadelphia: Hubbard Brothers, Publishers, 1886.

My Thirty Years Backstairs at the White House, Lillian Rogers Parks, in collaboration with Frances Spatz Leighton. New York: Fleet Publishing Corporation, 1961.

The White House, White House Historical Association, Washington, D.C., 1962.

White House Sailor, William M. Rigdon with James Derieux. Garden City, N.Y.: Doubleday & Company, Inc., 1962.

Profiles and Portraits of American Presidents, Margaret Bassett. New York: David McKay Company, Inc., 1964.

White House Brides, Marie Smith and Louise Durbin. Washington, D.C.: Acropolis Books, 1966.

Upstairs at the White House, J.B. West. New York: Coward, McCann & Geoghegan, Inc., 1973.

The Personal Memoirs of Julia Dent Grant, Mrs. Ulysses S. Grant. New York: Putnam, 1975 (originally written 1886–1892?).

Presidential Anecdotes, Paul F. Boller Jr. New York: Oxford University Press, 1981.

The President's House, Volumes I & II. William Seale. Washington, D.C.: White House Historical Association, 1986.

Presidential Wives, Paul F. Boller Jr. New York: Oxford University Press, 1988.

First Families, An Intimate Portrait from the Kennedys to the Clintons, Harry Benson. Boston: Little, Brown and Company, 1997.

America's First Families, Carl Anthony Sferrazza. New York: Simon & Schuster, 2000.

Real Life at the White House, John Whitcomb and Claire Whitcomb. New York: Routledge, 2000.

Hidden Power, Presidential Marriages that Shaped our Recent History, Kati Marton. New York: Pantheon Books, 2001.

Exclusively Presidential Trivia, Anthony S. Pitch. Potomac, Md.: Mino Publications, 2001.

Presidential Inaugurations, Paul F. Boller Jr. New York: Harcourt, Inc., 2001.

Flowers, White House Style, Dottie Temple and Stan Finegold. New York: Simon & Schuster, 2002.

A Treasury of Great American Scandals, Michael Farquhar. New York: Penguin Books, 2003.

The Quotable Founding Fathers, Buckner F. Melton Jr., editor. Washington, D.C.: Potomac Books, Inc., 2004.

First Families, Bonnie Angelo. New York: Harper Collins, 2005.

"I look forward to these confrontations with the press to kind of balance up the nice and pleasant things that come to me as President."

—Jimmy Carter

Index

INDEX OF RECIPES

Appetizers & Snacks
Cheese Wafers, Lady Bird Johnson, 158
Cream-Cheese Roll, Betty Ford, 169
Deviled Eggs, George W. and Laura Bush, 193
Fried Peanuts, Miss Lillian Carter, 173
Guacamole, Laura Bush, 195
Mexican Mound, Barbara Bush, 181
Nachos Special, Lady Bird Johnson, 158
Peanut Brittle, Carter Family, 173
Plains Special Cheese Ring, Rosalynn Carter, 170
Sausage Rolls, Caroline Harrison, 100
Shrimp Superb, Pat Nixon, 163
Smoked Shrimp with Mango Salsa, Laura Bush, 192
Spiced Nuts, 92
Tex-Mex Dip, Doro Bush Koch, 185
Trail Mix, Ronald Reagan, 174

Beverages
Bishop, Archbishop, or Pope, 59
Daniel Webster's Punch, 53
Eggnog, William Henry Harrison's Favorite, 49
Hot Chocolate, Laura Bush, 197
Lemonade Lucy's Lemonade, 86
Mint Juleps, Mount Vernon, 17
Raspberry Shrub, 56
Roman Punch, 83
Spiced Tea, LBJ Ranch, 160
Whiskey Sours, James Madison's Favorite, 28

Breads & Biscuits
Brown Bread, 99
Corn Bread, Lucy Hayes, 85
Corn Muffins, Ida McKinley, 104
Homemade Toasting Bread, Betty Ford, 168
Loyal Biscuits, 73
Monkey Bread, Nancy Reagan, 175
Popovers, 59
Sally Lunn, 52
Squash or Pumpkin Biscuit, Eleanor Roosevelt, 111
War Bread, 119
White Loaf Bread, Lucretia Garfield, 88

Breakfast Foods
Buckwheat Cakes, Martha Johnson Patterson, 77
Country Omelet, Richard Nixon's Favorite, 165
Rolled Toast, Lou Hoover, 128
Scarborough Puffs, 69

Scrambled Eggs, Eleanor Roosevelt, 132
Waffles, John Kennedy's Favorite, 152

Condiments & Sauces
Barbecue Sauce, Lyndon Johnson, 159
Chestnut Sauce, 67
Orange Jelly, 129
Orange Marmalade, Edith Roosevelt, 108
Raspberry Vinegar, 29
Salad Sauce, 43
Syrup of Roses, Elizabeth Monroe, 32
Tomato Sauce, 131
Wine Jelly, Ellen Wilson, 116

Cookies & Bars
Bird Seed Cookies, Jane Pierce, 64
Blarney Stones, Bess Truman, 139
Bourbon Balls, 122
Brownies, Bess Truman, 138
Chocolate Chip Cookies, Hillary Clinton, 188
Cookies, first published American cookie recipe, 43
Cowboy Cookies, Laura Bush, 195
Hedgehog Cookies, 41
Icebox Cookies, Grace Coolidge, 124
Kisses for a Slack Oven, 37
Macaroons, 24
Peanut Butter Cookies, Amy Carter, 172
Petticoat Tails, 31
Philadelphia Sand Tarts, Edith Roosevelt, 108
Waverly Jumbles, Monroe Family, 33

Desserts (also see Cookies & Bars and Puddings)
"A Dessert," Helen Taft, 114
A Dish of Snow, 65
Apple Pan Dowdy, Abigail Adams, 20
Arkansas Fried Pie, 189
Brandy Peaches, 30
Buttermilk Pie, Harry Truman's Favorite, 143
Charlotte Russe, "Woodrow's Favorite," 117
Coffee Soufflé, Grace Coolidge, 125
Courting Cake, Mary Lincoln, 70
Crème Brûlée, Jackie Kennedy, 153
Deacon Porter's Hat, 115
Deep Dish Apple Pie, Mamie Eisenhower, 149
Election Cake, 38
Frosting, Mary Lincoln, 71
Fudge, Mamie Eisenhower's Million Dollar, 146
Grant's Lemon Pie, 81
Great Cake, Martha Washington, 14

"Gyngerbrede," Mary Washington, 16
Harrison Cake, 48
Lemon Pie, Grace Coolidge, 124
Lincoln's Log, 75
Maids of Honor, 97
Modern adaptation of an 18th-century icing, 15
Pears in Cointreau with Frozen Cream, Ellen Wilson, 118
Pound Cake, Truman Family, 140
Scripture Cake, 57
Soufflé Froid au Chocolat, Jackie Kennedy, 155
Stuffed Lemon Dessert, Nancy Reagan, 177
Tipsy Watermelon, 107
White Layer Cake, Ida McKinley, 105

Entrées
Bass with Caper Sauce, 95
Beef Cooked with Peel of Mandarin Orange, Barbara Bush, 182
Beef Stew, Big Party, Dwight Eisenhower, 145
Beef Stew, Family-Size, Dwight Eisenhower, 145
Beef Stroganoff, Jackie Kennedy, 151
Boiled Salmon with Egg Sauce, 137
Bubble and Squeak, 99
Chicken Croquettes, Ida McKinley, 107
Chicken Enchiladas, Bill Clinton's Favorite, 187
Chinese Chop Suey, Lyndon Johnson, 157
Chinese Pepper Steak, Betty Ford, 167
Crabmeat Casserole, Nancy Reagan, 178
Curried Chicken, Mrs. James Roosevelt, 134
Curry of Lamb with Rice, Betty Ford, 166
Fillet de Boeuf Wellington, Pat Nixon, 162
Ham Roasted with Madeira, 44
Jambalaya, 60
Kedgeree, 133
Lancashire Pie, 79
Lemon Chicken, George H.W. Bush's Favorite, 180
Meat Loaf, Pat Nixon, 165
Meat Pasties, 21
Minted Chicken, 127
Oyster Stew, 87
Pork Chops with Spiced Apples, 50
Pot Roast, 63
Presidential Corned-Beef Hash, 131
Rissables, 90
Sacramento Chicken Pie, Nancy Reagan, 176
Squirrel Stew with Leftovers, 148
Veal and Bacon Pie, 17
Veal Cutlets in Papers, 25

Veal Olives, Julia Grant, 80
Venison, Lou Hoover, 128

Potatoes & Other Side Dishes (also see Vegetables)
Corn Fritters, 61
Eggplant Casserole, Carter Family, 171
Eggplant with Spaghetti or Rice, Alice Roosevelt
    Longworth, 109
Hominy Cheese Grits, 61
Hush Puppies, LBJ Ranch, 161
Macaroni, 27
Potatoes à la Duchesse, 66
Spoon Bread, 29
Sweet Potato Soufflé, Nancy Reagan, 174
Turkey Stuffing, Bess Truman, 142

Puddings (for Side Dishes and Dessert)
Bird's Nest Pudding, 49
Chestnut Flummery, 67
Fig Pudding, Caroline Harrison, 102
Hasty Pudding, 22
Ozark Pudding, Truman Family, 141
Pease Pudding, 46
Plum Pudding, 36
Sweet Potato Pudding, Eliza Johnson, 76
"Tyler's Pudding," 52
Union Pudding, 73

Salads
Bing Cherry Salad Mold, Bess Truman, 140
Bird's Nest Salad, 121
Chicken Salad, 55
"Cold" Slaw, 89
Cucumber Pickles, Elizabeth Monroe, 34
Cucumber Salad, 82
Eggplant Salad, 121
French Pickles, 84
Grape Salad, Rachel Jackson, 40
Potato Chip Salad, Pat Nixon, 164
Potato Salad, Dwight Eisenhower, 146
Runnymede Salad, 112
Salade à la Volaille, 44
Vegetable Salad, Barbara Bush, 184

Sandwiches
Elvis' Sandwich, 186
Sandwiches for Travelers, 42
Toasted Cheese Sandwich, Eleanor Roosevelt, 132

Soups
Carrot Vichyssoise, Betty Ford, 167

Chicken Soup à L'Amande, 135
Chili con Carne, Dwight Eisenhower, 144
Clear Soup, Caroline Harrison, 103
Colonial Peanut and Chestnut Soup, Mount
    Vernon, 19
Fish Chowder, Caroline Harrison, 101
Fish Chowder, John Kennedy's Favorite, 150
"Martha Washington's Crab Soup," 132
Mock Turtle Soup, Monroe Family, 35
Mulligatawny Soup, 94
Pedernales River Chili, Lyndon Johnson, 156
Senate Bean Soup, 120
Vegetable Soup, Laura Bush, 196

Vegetables
Arkansas Fried Green Tomatoes, 190
Asparagus with Eggs, 93
Baked Tomatoes, 49
Boston Baked Beans, 39
Caramel Tomatoes, 130
Cauliflowers, 62
Mushrooms in Cream, 18
Peas, Green, 47
Sauerkraut, 68
Spinach Parmesan, Lady Bird Johnson, 160
Stewed Beets, Martin Van Buren's Favorite, 45
Vegetable Chartreuse, 26
Yummy Green Beans, Barbara Bush, 183

GENERAL INDEX

A
Acheson, Mrs. Dean, 139
Allen, George, 165
Adams, Abigail, 20, 21, 23, 62
Adams, Charles, 37
Adams, George, 37
Adams, John, 20-23, 160, 192, 198
Adams, John (son of John Quincy Adams), 37
Adams, John Quincy, 36-39, 192, 198
Adams, Louisa, 36, 37
Adams National Historical Park, 36
Air Force One, 170
Alabama, 69
American Cookery, 22, 43
American Frugal Housewife, The, 49, 56
American Home Cook Book, The, 62, 82
American House Wife Cook Book, The, 75
American Revolution, 25
Ames, Mary Clemmer, 75
Andover, 194

Antoinette, Marie, 35
Arkansas, 189, 190
Army Wife's Cookbook, An, 73
Aronson, Virginia, 168
Art of Cookery Made Plain and Easy, The, 21
Arthur, Chester A., 91, 92-95, 198
Ash-Lawn Highland, 32-35

B
Baby Ruth (Cleveland), 98
Baer, Jacob, 68
Bailyn, Bernard, 191
Barbecue, 18, 48, 147, 159
Barkley, Alben, 142
Barlow, Joel, 22
Battle of New Orleans, 42
Bedtime for Bonzo, 175
Beecher, Catharine, 65, 69
Beeches, The, 127
Benton, Jessie, 43
Benton, Senator Thomas, 43
Bible, 23, 57, 62
Black, Mrs. Hugo, 139
Blair-Lee House, 143
Bliss, Betty, 60
Blue Room, 34, 45, 74, 86, 96, 186
Booth, John Wilkes, 11, 75
Bostwick, Lucy, 81
"Breakfast Dish," 122
Buchanan, James, 66-69, 198
Buckingham Palace, 136
Buckley, Katherine, 131
Bush, Barbara, 180-185, 186, 188
Bush, Barbara (daughter of George W. Bush), 197
Bush Family Cookbook, The, 185
Bush, George H.W., 180-185, 189, 192, 199
Bush, George W., 192-197, 199
Bush, Jenna, 197
Bush, Laura, 192-197

C
California, 163, 176
Camp David, 149, 175, 185
Campbell Soup, 106
Cannon, "Uncle Joe," 120
Canton Favorite Cook Book, The, 104, 105, 107
Capitol Hill, 120, 187
Card, Andy, 197
Carr, Vietta, 141
Carter, Amy, 172, 173
Carter, Chip, 173

Carter, Jack, 173
Carter, Jimmy, 170-173, 189, 199
Carter, Jeff, 173
Carter, Miss Lillian, 170, 173
Carter, Rosalynn, 170, 171, 173
Cassini, Countess, 109
Centennial Exposition, 81
Century Cook Book, The, 121
Century Magazine, The, 89
Chambrin, Pierre, 187
Cheney, Lynne, 196, 197
Cherry Trees (in Washington), 112
Child, Lydia Maria, 49, 56
Christmas, 27, 41, 85, 103, 108, 109, 129, 161
Churchill, Winston, 137
Civil War, 69, 74, 77
"Clam Soup Poem," 65
Clark, Allen C., 29
Clay, Mrs. Clement, 69
Clay, Henry, 45, 56
Cleveland, Francis, 98
Cleveland, Grover, 10, 96-99, 198
Cleveland, Rose, 96
Clinton, Chelsea, 189
Clinton, Hillary Rodham, 186-188, 191
Clinton, William J., 186-191, 199
Coalter, Mrs. Frances, 30
Cockburn, British Admiral, 30
Comerford, Cristeta, 193, 197
Congress, 21, 30, 33, 62, 77, 82, 87, 93, 102, 177
Constitution, 28
Cook's Own Book and Housekeeper's Register, The, 42, 43, 44, 47
Coolidge, Calvin, 124-127, 199
Coolidge, Grace, 124-127
Cooper, James Fenimore, 33
Cornelius, Mary, 48
Cox, Edward Finch, 164
Crook, Colonel, 85
Custis, Frances Parke, 17, 18
Custis, Nellie, 18

D

Daily Star, The, 120
Declaration of Independence, 30
De Guzman, Ariel, 182, 185
Democratic National Convention, 188
"Directions for Making a CHOUDER," 151
Dixie Cook Book, 78
Dole, Elizabeth, 188
Dole, Sanford B., 106

Donelson, Emily, 40
Dove, Rita, 191

E

East Room, 23, *77,* 89, 101, 102, 110, 112, 118, 136, 139, 161, 165, 169
Easter Egg Rolling, 87
Economy Administration Cook Book, The, 117
18th Amendment, 123
Eisenhower, Dwight D., 144-149, 199
Eisenhower, Mamie, 139, 144, 146, 149, 160
Eisenhower, Milton, 147
Election Day, 38
Ellington, Duke, 163
England, 52, 136, 137
Evarts, William M., 86
"Eve's Pudding," 46

F

Family Circle, 188
Farmer, Fannie Merritt, 112
Fields, Alonzo, 130, 140
Fife and Drum Corps, 154
Fillmore, Abigail Powers, 62
Fillmore, Mary Abigail, 62
Fillmore, Millard, 62, 63, 198
First Baptist Church, Canton, Ohio, 104, 105, 107
First Presbyterian Church, Galena, Illinois, 11, 80
Fleischer, Ari, 197
Florida, 60, 142
Folsom, Frances (Frank), 96
Ford, Betty, 166-169
Ford, Gerald, 166-169, 189, 199
Ford's Theatre, 11, 75
4-H Clubs, 129
Franklin Pierce Manse, 64

G

Gardiner, Julia, 55
Garfield, James A., 88-91, 198
Garfield, Lucretia, 88, 89
Gautier's of Washington, 66
Georgia, 107, 170, 171
Germany, 119
Girl Scouts, 129
Gillette, Mrs. F.L., 97, 99
Glasse, Hanna, 21
Godey's Lady's Book, 48, 73, 90
Golf, 113, 148
Gonzales, Alberto, 197
Grabner, Ted, 177

Grant, Julia, 11, 80-83
Grant, Nellie, 83
Grant, Ulysses S., 10, 80-83, 198
Great Depression, 133
Greenbrier Resort, 187
Gridiron Club, 137
Grierson, Alice K., 73
Guiteau, Charles, 91

H

Hagin, Joseph, 194
"Hail to the Chief," 150
Haller, Henry, 163, 168, 177
Harding, Florence, 120-123
Harding, Warren G., 120-123, 199
Harrison, Anna, 51
Harrison, Benjamin, 51, 100-103, 123, 199
Harrison, Benny, 101
Harrison, Caroline, 100-103
Harrison, William Henry, 47, 48-51, 198
Harvard University, 118
Hass, Robert, 191
Hastings, General Russell, 86
Havel, Václav, 191
Hawaii, 76, 106
Hawking, Stephen, 191
Hayes, Lucy, 10, 84-87
Hayes, Rutherford B., 84-87, 198
Helen, Mary Catherine, 37
Hemingway, Ernest, 134
Henderson, Mary F., 86, 87
Hepburn, Audrey, 174
"Herb Sallad for the Tavern Bowl, An", 50
Herbert Hoover Presidential Library, 128-131
Hermitage, The, 40
Herndon, Billy, 70
Heston, Charlton, 174
Hightower, Harry T., 143
Hiram College, 91
Hockersmith, Kaki, 186
Holmes, Oliver Wendell, 84
Hoover, Herbert, 128-131, 199
Hoover, Herbert Jr., 129
Hoover, Lou Henry, 128-131
Hoover, Millie, 131
Hotel del Coronado, 163
House Beautiful, 186
House of Representatives, 36, 91
"Housekeeper's Alphabet," 78
House-Keeper's Pocket-Book, The, 21
"How to Preserve a Husband," 54

I

Ice Cream, 31, 36
Inonu, Ismet, 160
Invitation to the White House, An, 186
Iowa, 131
Irving, Washington, 31
Italy, 24

J

Jackson, Andrew, 11, 40-43, 58, 110, 160, 198
Jackson, Rachel, 40, 41
Jefferson, Martha, 25
Jefferson, Thomas, 24-27, 30, 160, 178, 198
Jelly Beans, 179
Jetton, Walter, 159
Jimmy Carter Presidential Library, 171, 173
John Adams' Recipe to Make a Patriot, 20
Johnson, Andrew, 75, 76-79, 198
Johnson, Eliza, 76, 79
Johnson, Lady Bird, 156-161, 189
Johnson, Luci Baines, 156, 161
Johnson, Lynda Bird, 161
Johnson, Lyndon B., 156-161, 163, 199

K

Keene, Laura, 10, 75
Kennedy, Caroline, 152
Kennedy, Jacqueline, 151-155, 156
Kennedy, John F., 150-155, 199
Kennedy, John Jr., 152
Kennedy, Joseph, 155
Kentucky, 70, 71
Khan, Ayub, 154
King George VI, 136
King, Rufus, 69
Kissinger, Henry, 171, 191
Koch, Doro Bush, 185

L

Lafayette, General, 16, 37
Lane, Harriett, 66, 69
Lee, Robert E., 74
Lenox China, 177, 189
Leslie, Eliza, 16, 42, 43, 44, 47
Lewis and Clark, 26
Library of Congress, 29
Life and Letters of Dolley Madison, 29
Lincoln, Abraham, 10, 11, 17, 69, 70-75, 143, 193, 198
Lincoln, Mary Todd, 70, 71, 75
Lincoln, Tad, 72, 74

Lincoln, Willie, 74
Literary Society of Washington, 89
Little White House, 142
London, 52, 136
Longfellow, Henry Wadsworth, 84
Longworth, Alice Roosevelt, 109
Louisiana, 60

M

Madison, Dolley, 25, 28-31, 45, 58, 87
Madison, James, 18, 28-31, 198
Maine, 182
Marcos, Ferdinand and Imelda, 160
Margery Daw in the Kitchen, 81
Marine Band, 41, 64, 74, 96, 121, 157
Market Square Tavern Kitchen, 31
Maryland, 149
Marsalis, Wynton, 191
Massachusetts, 46, 127, 139
McAdoo, William Gibbs, 118
McElroy, Mary, 92
McKinley, Ida, 104, 105, 107
McKinley, William, 11, 104-107, 199
McPartland, Marian, 191
Meese, Ed, 174
Mesnier, Roland R., 177, 193
Mexican War, 60
Millennium Evenings, 191
Minthorn, Mary Wasley, 129
Miss Beecher's Domestic Receipt Book, 65, 69
Mitterand, Francois and Mrs., 179
Monroe, Elizabeth, 10, 32-35
Monroe, James, 32-35, 47, 160, 198
Monroe, Maria, 34
Montgomery, John R., 40
Monticello, 25, 26, 27, 30
Montpelier, 28
Morton, Levi, 102
Mount Holyoke College, 115
Mount Vernon, 15, 66, 154
Mount Vernon Ladies Association, 17, 19

N

National Building Museum, 90
Native Americans, 29
National Shrine of the Immaculate Conception, 161
National Symphony Orchestra, 154, 157
Navy Times, 143
Nesbitt, Henrietta, 134, 135, 137
New Art of Cookery, 49
New Book of Cookery, 112

New Hampshire, 65
New Jersey, 116
New York, 36, 55, 81, 108, 110, 111, 136, 187
New York City Ballet, 157
New York Times, 106
Newsday, 162
"Nice Indian Pudding, A", 22
Nixon, Hannah Milhous, 164
Nixon, Pat, 162-165
Nixon, Richard M., 162-165, 166, 199
Nixon, Tricia, 164
North Portico, 41
Northwest Territory, 60

O

Octagon House, 30
Ohio, 51, 84, 87, 89
Ordaz, Gustavo Diaz, 163
Our American Cousin, 11, 75
Our Own Cook Book, 11, 80
Oval Office, 152, 182

P

Page, Walter Hines, 116
Panic of 1837, 47
Paris, 24, 27, 131
Patterson, Martha Johnson, 76-79
Payne, Anna, 69
Pearson, Lester, 150
Pearson, Mrs. Lester, 139
Pennsylvania, 68
Pentagon, 163
Philadelphia, 36, 66, 108
Philippines, 113
Pierce, Franklin, 64, 65, 180, 198
Pierce, Jane, 64
Pinsker, Mathew, 72
Pinsky, Robert, 191
Pitts, Milton, 180
Platt, Emily, 86
Polk, James K., 56-59, 198
Polk, Sarah, 56, 58, 59
Pond House, 170
Potomac River, 39, 66, 154, 158, 190
Practical Cooking and Dinner Giving, 10, 85, 86, 87
Presbyterian Cook Book, The, 89
Presidential Cookbook, The, 135, 137
Presidential Medal of Freedom, 163
Presley, Elvis, 186
Prince Albert, 66
Prince Charles, 177

Princeton University, 116
Putin, Vladimir, 194

Q

"Quarreling Recipe," 73
Queen Emma, 76
Queen Elizabeth, 136
Queen Victoria, 62

R

Ratley, Mary, 130
Rayburn, Sam, 142
Reagan, Michael, 178
Reagan, Nancy, 174-179
Reagan, Ronald, 163, 174-179, 199
Rhode Island, 95
Rice, Condoleezza, 194
Rock Creek Horse Center, 175
Rock Creek Park, 76, 148
Rogers, Maggie, 116
Ronald, Mary, 121
Roosevelt, Anna, 137
Roosevelt, Archie, 109, 110
Roosevelt, Edith, 108, 111
Roosevelt, Eleanor, 129, 132-137, 138
Roosevelt, Franklin D., 23, 132-137, 149, 166, 199
Roosevelt, Mrs. James, 134
Roosevelt, Quentin, 110
Roosevelt, Theodore, 108-111, 113, 127, 166, 199
Root, Elihu, 113
Rose Garden, 157, 164
Royall, Anne, 39
Russia, 36, 163
Rutherford B. Hayes Presidential Center, 10, 84, 85

S

Sagamore Hill National Historic Site, 108, 111
Saltonstall, Mrs. Leverett, 139
Sandwich Islands, 76
Sayre, Francis P., 118
Scheib, Walter, 187
Seaton, Mrs. William, 34
Secret Service, 119, 123, 136, 142, 161, 180, 183, 187, 190
Senate, 55, 91, 115
Seventy-Five Recipes for Pastry, Cakes and Sweetmeats, 16
Shakespeare, 74
Sheep (on White House Lawn), 119
Short, William, 27
Shute, Miss T.S., 75

Simmons, Amelia, 22, 43
Sinatra, Frank, 163, 174
Smith College, 181
Smith, Margaret Bayard, 28
Smith, Sidney, 50
Sousa, John Philip, 96
South Lawn, 113, 173
Spiegel Grove, 87
Springwood, 136
Stanton, Elizabeth W., 122
State Dining Room, 23, 40, 41, 83, 109, 110, 117, 139, 160, 189
Statesmen's Dishes and How to Cook Them, 100-103
Stowe, Harriet Beecher, 65
Stuart, Gilbert, 30

T

Taft, Charlie, 110
Taft, Helen (daughter of William Taft), 112
Taft, Helen (wife of William Taft), 112-115
Taft, William H., 112-115, 199
Taylor, Margaret, 60
Taylor, Zachary, 60, 61, 198
Tennessee, 40, 76, 79
Texas, 55, 159, 161, 185, 192, 194
Thanksgiving, 74, 85, 115
Tiffany and Co., 154, 156
Tiffany, Louis Comfort, 93
Tokyo, 112
Treatise on Domestic Economy, A, 65
Truman, Bess, 138-141
Truman, Harry, 138-143, 199
Truman, Margaret, 141
Tucker, St. George, 30
Tyler, John, 52-55, 198
Tyler, John Jr., 55
Tyler, Julia, 55
Tyler, Letitia, 53
Tyler, Priscilla, 53
Tyler, Robert, 53

U

University of Texas, 192
U.S. Capitol, 48, 70, 87
Utley, Dr. Vine, 26

V

Val-Kill Cottage, 136
Van Buren, Angelica, 45
Van Buren, Martin, 11, 44-47, 180, 198
Vallette, Maria, 84

Vinson, Fred and Mrs., 142
Virginia, 28, 31, 33, 119
Vonnegut, Kurt, 191

W

Walker's Point, 182
War of 1812, 33, 42
Washington, George, 14-19, 30, 132, 154, 198
Washington, Martha, 14, 17, 132
Washington, Mary, 16, 17
Washington Redskins, 165
Washington Star, The, 71
Wayne, John, 163
Webster, Daniel, 53
Wellesley College, 181
West, J.B., 138, 149
West Virginia, 48
West Wing, 110
Wheatland, 68
White House China Collection, 100
White House Cook Book, The, 10, 12, 97, 99
White House Family Cookbook, The, 168
White House fires, 30, 45, 127, 161
White House Gang, 110
White House greenhouses, 71, 104
White House library, 62
White, William Allen, 116
Whittier, John Greenleaf, 84
Wiesel, Elie, 191
Wilcox, Estelle Woods, 78
William McKinley Presidential Library & Museum, 104, 105, 107
Willingham, Martha, 77
Wilson, Edith, 119
Wilson, Eleanor, 118
Wilson, Ellen, 116-118
Wilson, Jessie, 118
Wilson, Mrs. Joseph, 117
Wilson, Woodrow, 116-119, 199
Wise, John S., 92
Woman Suffrage Cook Book, The, 122
Woodrow Wilson House, The, 119
World War I, 119
World War II, 133, 136, 147, 154

Y

Yale University, 194
Young Housekeeper's Friend, The, 48

Z

Ziemann, Hugo, 10, 97, 99